# REPS!

## —The World's Hottest Bodybuilding Routines!—

# REPS!

## The World's Hottest Bodybuilding Routines!

# ROBERT
# KENNEDY

Sterling Publishing Co., Inc.   New York

**Edited by Robert Hernandez**
**Designed by Jim Anderson**

**Library of Congress Cataloging-in-Publication Data**

Kennedy, Robert, 1938—
    Reps! : the world's hottest bodybuilding routines!

    Includes index.
    1. Bodybuilding.    I. Title.
GV546.5.K462 1985      646.7'5      85-17223
ISBN 0-8069-6250-X (pbk.)

# CONTENTS

# APPRECIATION

Writing a book is always a group effort. I owe a debt of thanks to Ken Wheeler, owner of the Super Fitness Gym in Toronto; to Joe Gold, owner of the World Gym; to Eric and Marsha Levine, owners of Gold's Gym in Toronto; to Louis Miua of the Universe Gym; to Jack Niehausen of Gold's Gym in Thornhill; to Peter Grymkowski, owner of Gold's Gym in California; to the Golden Fitness Club in Scarborough, Canada.

A special word of appreciation to Joe and Ben Weider for giving me a free hand at their prestigious IFBB shows; to Wayne and Karen DeMilia for assigning me a good spot on which to set up my camera.

Thanks to Robert Hernandez, my editor at Sterling Publishing Co., Inc.; to Steve Douglas, who not only took many of the photos, but also designed the cover and did the illustrations for this book.

Among the photographers I would like to acknowledge: Mike Read, my custom processor, and the capable photographic work of Garry Bartlett, Tapio Hautala, John Balik, Chris Lund, Edward Hankey, Russ Warner, Bob Gruskin, Bob Flippin, Peter Potter, John Campos, Jim Marchand, Robert Nailon, Wayne Gallasch, Paul B. Goode, Lance Mitchell, Andy Cushing, Geoff Collins, Denie Walter, Doris Barrilleaux, Al Antuck, George Greenwood, Gino Edwards, Reg Bradford, Bill Heimanson, Monty Heron, Bill Reynolds, Roger Shelley, Doug White, and Art Zeller. Thank you one and all.

Kevin Lawrence and Diana Dennis

# INTRODUCTION

There are people who believe that the perfect bodybuilding routine exists somewhere, the all-encompassing workout schedule that is guaranteed to give them the perfect body in the shortest amount of time. In fact, no such routine exists for one very simple reason: The body—its needs, reactions, and metabolic processes—is in a constant state of change. Accordingly, the method you use to stimulate reaction has to change with the needs of your body.

Whether you want to add size, gain muscle, lose weight, increase definition, or improve fitness, the routine has to be specially tailored to the task at hand.

This book—more than any other previously published work—dissects, examines, and reconstructs the workout routine. You will soon discover that a personally designed weight-training routine, using progressive-resistance exercise, has a single purpose: *to stimulate and develop your body.* The purpose of this book is to present you with the best training information available. You are in for a real treat with this book. Not only will you learn all the training variations and important aspects of sets and repetitions, you'll also discover the latest theories about the winning edge, workout frequency, and exercise performance.

The ultimate reason for taking this mega-dose of bodybuilding information, the thing that makes this book the best yet, is the first-time presentation in the history of the Iron Game of *the hottest training routines ever compiled by man, woman, or computer.*

From this day onwards, you are going to succeed in your training goals. Yes, you can bet your barbell that things are going to get better.

Follow the advice in this book and your body will reflect the difference faster than you can spell *Schwarzenegger.* Let's go!

*Rich Gaspari, IFBB World Champion*

# Part 1

# WHAT IS A ROUTINE?

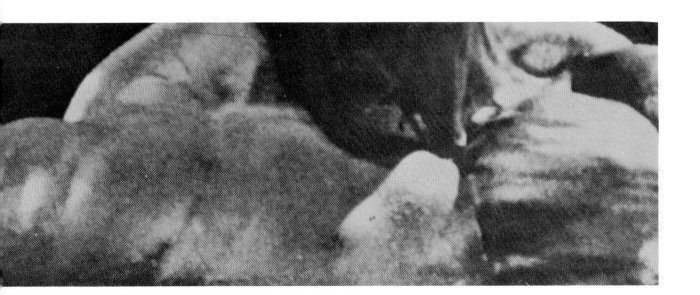

*Bob Paris*

**O**ut of all the hundreds of thousands of bodybuilders currently pumping iron, very few are using the correct routine to achieve superior results. It has often been said that a missed workout can never be made up. The same goes for a workout that is not designed to give you the best possible physique.

Before a routine is adopted or formulated, you should be sure that it is the correct routine for you. For example, a person who wants overall fitness and cardiovascular efficiency would *not* be doing the most advantageous routine if he or she follows a heavy powerlift-ing workout. Likewise a person desiring maximum bulk will not achieve much if he practices a circuit-training program.

Are you currently progressing to achieve your bodybuilding goals? If you get no results from your training, then you are wasting your time. There is far more to a routine than merely a list of exercises. Also of vital importance is the amount of sets, repetitions or "reps," the degree of intensity, tempo, style, mental attitude, capacity for development, not to mention the choice of equipment. These are just a few of the topics that are covered in this first part of your quest to develop a more muscular body.

*Bodybuilders work out at Gold's Gym in Venice, California.*

# CUSTOMIZING YOUR WORKOUT

Bodybuilding beginners who join a gym, or who start training at home, invariably make some quick progress. The very fact that they are suddenly shocking their bodies with progressive-resistance exercise is enough to sur-

prise those muscles into reacting in some way. Growth results. Tone improves. Strength increases.

However, the fundamental question of how weight training affects the physique remains a matter of great controversy. There is an annual pilgrimage to Southern California (usually to Gold's and World's gyms) by men and women from all over the world. Their plight? To find out the best method to train! They want to be up to date and know all the "secrets."

Actually, they invariably end up more confused than ever. Recently there has been an explosion of theories regarding how to train to get *more* results in *less* time. Remember the old theory: *low reps for strength and size— high reps for definition and shape?* It's no longer that simple, and even that training philosophy has become outdated.

Today we have different schools of thought, each offering its own rationale: the Nautilus principles pioneered by Arthur Jones, the heavy-duty system of Mike Mentzer, the shaping routines of Vince Gironda, the high-set routines of Arnold Schwarzenegger and Frank Zane, the extended sets of Tom Platz, who combined Mentzer's and Schwarzenegger's methods. There are scores more. All will be explained in this book.

Even though training methods differ greatly, all the bodybuilding champions have one thing in common. They have achieved physique greatness, and proved it on the posing platform. Gladys Portugues, Rachel McLish, Corinna Everson, Arnold Schwarzenegger, Lee Haney, Mohamed Makkawy, Mike Mentzer, Frank Zane, and many more.

Out of all this comes one major fact. There is no single best way to train. As Bill Dobbins, a well-known writer in the bodybuilding field, put it:

There is an equation consisting of a number of variables (i.e., sets, reps, frequency, amount of weight, tempo, etc.), all of which can be altered significantly, as long as the two sides of the equation remain in balance. The champions who train differently are merely solving the same equation in a different way, all of them arriving at the same result, a prize-winning physique.

Having accepted this philosophy, it now remains to conclude whether every champion is actually achieving greatness with maximum efficiency, or are they putting out more effort than they need to achieve identical results?

This reminds me of how the Mike Mentzer/Arnold Schwarzenegger feud came about. When Arnold was winning his consecutive Mr. Olympia titles (1970–1975), he was doing very well financially by selling his training manuals, each of which advocated plenty of sets and reps and hard work, a philosophy which Arnold had always followed personally. Then came Mentzer with his heavy-duty philosophy, advocating people to train harder, but less. Ul-timately, he was saying: Why spend three or four hours in the gym every day when 45 minutes every *other* day, working with maximum intensity, will give superior results.

At a seminar that Mike Mentzer was holding, a specific question arose. It was to become asked at almost every seminar that Mentzer gave. "If your heavy-duty methods are so good, how come Arnold Schwarzenegger doesn't use them?"

Not wanting to put down his colleague, Mentzer at first avoided making an issue of the matter. Initially, he passed it off as "each to his own." Eventually, as the questions became a regular at every Mentzer seminar, Mike

*Arnold Schwarzenegger coaches Jusup Wilkosz in a squat exercise.*

couldn't resist changing his answer from one that avoided unnecessary conflict with Arnold to one that challenged the Austrian's very authority on training. In essence, he said: "If Arnold had used my methods, he would have been even better!"

Now the war was on. When Arnold found out that Mentzer was publicly deriding his training philosophy, he countered by showing his contempt for Mentzer's heavy-duty methods.

As time progressed, Mentzer entered the 1979 Mr. Olympia (run by Arnold) in Columbus, Ohio, and in spite of being at his all-time best, Mike was beaten out for the top spot by traditionalist-trainer Frank Zane.

The following year in Australia, Arnold actually entered the 1980 Mr. Olympia contest, as a last-minute surprise, and he won the title, much to the chagrin of Mentzer and others who felt that Arnold was not at his best. They believed that the judges looked at him and recalled his six previous Mr. Olympia titles. Of course, whether Arnold was at *his* best is totally irrelevant. What is to be considered is whether he had the best physique on stage.

Time is of the essence, especially to an aspiring young bodybuilder. Accordingly, *your* level of efficiency is extremely important. Training efficiency is defined as the degree of success that follows the degree of effort. In other words, it is how much you get out of your training compared to the energy and time you put into it. After you surpass the beginner's stage, every additional pound of muscle mass becomes harder to develop. But you can continue to make gains, even from methods that are not 100 percent efficient. It could be argued that many champions have taken the long route to success, when, in fact, they could have used fully efficient short-cut methods to achieve greatness, had they known of them.

*Your* job comes down to this: You need the information in these pages to customize your workouts to attain your goals as much as is humanly possible. As progress is made, your training needs will change. No two days of training are ever identical, but it is up to you to keep informed of your progress, needs, and goals so that you can make changes in your routine to keep results coming.

# TRAINING INTENSITY

The bottom line of training intensity is to increase the work load of an exercise. However, there are scores of ways of increasing intensity without adding more weight. Mike Mentzer's philosophy encompasses the scientific conclusion that a muscle increases in size when it is regularly subjected to a greater load. The other basic variable that goes hand in hand with increased weight is the time factor. Lift the same amount of weight in *less* time and you will have increased workout intensity.

Mike Mentzer believes in training with maximum weight.

*NABBA Mr. Universe Jeff King*

Weightlifters as well as bodybuilders use this progressive-resistance principle, but they use lower repetitions, not being interested in gaining excessive muscle size, as is the case with the competitive bodybuilder. As a male bodybuilder trying to obtain 20-inch arms, or a woman trying for 14 inches, high-intensity training will form an important part of your workouts. Unlike the weightlifter, however, your repetitions should be between eight and twelve.

*Erika Mes of Holland performs an upright row.*

*Australian John Terilli curls dumbbells on an incline bench.*

The higher reps are important because of the unique way they affect muscle fibre. You need a certain amount of repetitions to build additional muscle fibre. High-intensity workouts, whereby you attempt to increase the weights for every workout, are *theoretically* ideal; however, other factors come into the picture. A bodybuilder can quickly "burn out" using such techniques after a month or two, and there is some evidence to show that substantial sets (more than the one or two sets advocated by the heavy-duty method) are needed to maximize muscle size. More sets and reps can also increase the body's capacity to supply blood to the fibres and enable the body to store more glycogen (carbohydrate energy) in the muscles.

The way in which you lift weights or exercise on a machine is known as your training style or form. It breaks down into two categories, good or strict style, and poor or cheating style. Ironically, even the so-called poor method of exercising has its place in modern bodybuilding. Trainer Vince Gironda named it *creative cheating*. Others call it loose exercise style. The technique has been used by every bodybuilder at one time or another. The most success seems to come to those who use it only when they cannot benefit from using good form in an exercise.

For those new to bodybuilding, cheating is a method of lifting a weight by using additional body motion or a larger muscle group to complete each repetition. For example, a cheat curl is one whereby you lean forward as you start to curl the barbell, bend your arms, and then as the weight rises you lean rearwards to take advantage of the momentum.

A cheat bench press involves the raising of the hips as the weight goes up. One who cheats in the squatting exercise will bounce from the low squat position in order to stand up with the weight.

When you train with good exercise style, you work a muscle through its entire range of motion. When you use cheating methods, you involve other larger muscles to help out. These muscles gain nothing from the action. However, because they have been brought in to help, the easiest part of an exercise—when performed strictly—may become the hardest part when cheating is involved. In other words, creative cheating can be a positive aid, but you need to know *how much* to cheat, and more importantly, *when*. (See page 57.)

Arnold Schwarzenegger invariably used very strict exercise form during the first eight repetitions of an exercise, and when he could not do another rep he would resort to controlled cheating. Thus he gained the value of both techniques, but only after he had exhausted the benefits of eight quality repetitions in perfect exercise style.

Only a fool would insist that his performance in every workout beat out the previous one. To follow such a regimen would be psychologically and physiologically damaging. However, efforts at increasing weight progression have to be practiced regularly, if not quite all the time. New plateaus of achievement are only attained when you actively *reach* for them.

Applying the overload principle to your training means that you have to either in-

Ming Chew of New York City

crease intensity, decrease time between sets, or increase the amount of sets performed. Each successive set taxes the muscle in a way that the previous set did not. What prevents us from doing hundreds of sets of each exercise is our limited *energy* reserves, the time factor, and most importantly, our recuperation mechanism. It's no good doing 20 sets of heavy squats if you take a couple of weeks to recover from them!

*Berry DeMey shows good form in a seated dumbbell triceps extension.*

Progression should be achieved in small steps. Do not suddenly throw yourself into a high-intensity overload workout. You could end up feeling very nauseated. Ease into it slowly. Overenthusiasm can lead the unsuspecting bodybuilder to a deterioration in proper exercise style just for the sake of increasing weights.

# EXERCISE ORDER AND WEIGHT

The order in which you do your exercises is important, although some authorities would have you believe otherwise. Even though there are exceptions (i.e., the Peripheral Heart Action [P.H.A.] routine), you tend to work the large muscle areas first in a routine, when you have maximum energy, tapering off to the lighter (smaller) areas as the schedule progresses. Few people would feel like ending a long routine with eight sets of gruelling squats!

Most workouts are concluded with abdominal work or arm training, because neither places great demands on our energy reserves.

The great majority of bodybuilders begin their routines with the bench press. It's by far the most comfortable exercise to do and seems to warm up the body in just the right way. You are gradually coaxed into vigorous performance as more and more weight is added to the bar. Squats invariably follow chest work (if you are training legs and chest on the same day). You certainly can't leave heavy leg training until late in your routine. It's too demanding a movement.

On page 73, I explain the muscle-priority system of training, whereby you first work the area that most needs attention. In other words, train your weakest area first while your energy level is high, and you can give the most effort to the exercises. The reasoning appears sound, although I have personally noticed that very few champions actually follow the muscle-priority system, preferring to begin with a favorite exercise.

One of the most important aspects of correct order in your routine is to keep the exercises for one general area grouped together. For example, follow the bench press with one or more other exercises for the chest. Don't do one exercise for the chest, then one for the back, followed by a leg exercise, and finally back to the chest. The idea is to work one area hard, usually with several movements, break down as much muscle tissue as possible, and then move onto the next muscle area. This technique used to be known as *flushing* and was publicized greatly by Joe Weider in the 1960s, but it is not mentioned so much nowadays. It is, however, commonly used by all champions—men and women—and its value is never questioned.

The amount of weight that you use in an exercise must be sufficient to stimulate the muscles, yet not so much as to cause you to use excessively sloppy form. Neither must it be so heavy that you cannot complete your allocated repetitions for a given exercise. While every safety precaution should be taken to guard against injury, you should not baby yourself, either. Develop enough physical stamina to handle heavy weights in your workout.

It could be argued that the amount of weight you use is irrelevant because the body doesn't know how heavy a weight is during an exercise. And certainly, by performing an exercise in an ultrastrict fashion, you can make a relatively light weight *seem* heavy, and reap the same benefits of heavier resistance.

There is, of course, an answer to all this conjecture. You must use a weight light enough to allow you to train in good style, while heavy enough to fully tax the muscles being exercised. Beginners, of course, should favor relatively light weights, rather than struggle with weights that are heavy.

Even advanced bodybuilders are aware that there are some exercises that defy heavy weights, such as upright rows, triceps kickbacks, front and posterior deltoid raises, and straight-arm pullovers. Such exercises are not beneficial if excessively heavy weights are used.

*Vera Bendel of Germany*

*Samir Bannout and Jusup Wilkosz*

# WORKOUT LENGTH

Once you're training your body with progressive-resistance exercise, you should gradually attempt to make the most of your workout time. No one wants to spend unnecessary time in a gym!

The philosophy is to build up to the point where, during each workout, you train hard and heavy, with minimum rest between sets. You must train aggressively. Train each muscle group to the limit and then move onwards.

Beginners should not train for more than 40 minutes, and even advanced bodybuilders should not work out for more than two hours. Marathon workouts drain your glycogen levels, depleting your energy. If you repeatedly lengthen your workouts (a very easy thing to do), then you will get yourself into a situation where you will run out of energy, putting a strain on your entire nervous system, all of which interferes with your natural recuperation. As Mr. Olympia Samir Bannout said:

You have to train hard and concentrate. And you have to be smart. Your allotted time and energy are actually quite limited, and you have to make the most of them. You can't waste time. My objective is a maximum pump. I go for it with a vengeance. I want to feel that muscle explode with blood!

As you advance in bodybuilding, there is a temptation (and often a need) to increase both the number of exercises you use, as well as the number of sets in each exercise. Both inevitably result in making your workouts longer. Rather than perform marathon workouts, bodybuilders are advised to split their routines in two, or even three sections, devoting entire workouts to just training certain parts of the body. (See page 84 for the specifics of splitting up your workout.)

There is very little agreement on how many exercises you should do in your workout. Certainly every exercise "hits" your muscles from a slightly different angle. Rational deduction would perhaps favor the use of just one set of each exercise, with a large number of exercises. In this way you pound the muscles from every conceivable angle, maximizing tone, growth, and shape. Mike Mentzer has adopted this type of training methodology. But rather than just doing one set of each exercise, he usually does two or even three. On the other side of the coin, Reg Park and Vince Gironda have both proclaimed the usefulness of employing just *one* good exercise for each body part, even for advanced bodybuilders.

The general method, although not carved in stone, is that *beginners* perform just *one* exercise for each body part, *intermediates* do *two* exercises for each area, and the *advanced* trainers perform *three* or even *four* different exercises for each body part.

There are several factors to consider when determining the number of exercises to do in a workout. Since it is far better to undertrain than overtrain, you must never do so many exercises that you cannot fully recuperate by your next workout. Finally, there's the point of whether or not a certain body part actually *needs* a great amount of stimulation. We all have areas of our bodies that respond well to exercise (and others that are not so responsive).

*Brian Homka pumps out the last rep while Scott Wilson urges him on.*

Mr. Olympia Franco Columbu

# HOW MANY REPS?

Writing in *Muscle & Fitness* magazine, Franco Columbu said:

Best bodybuilding results will be derived if the reps are kept between eight and twelve. Anything less than six repetitions of an exercise will not impose a demand upon the body's reserve abilities sufficient to stimulate any worthwhile response. Too many reps, more than fifteen, will probably tax the cardiorespiratory system more than the muscular system.

Bodybuilders, young and old, are always looking for the answer to the question: *How many reps?* There is no single ideal number. You could make great progress using a system of twelve reps for each exercise, only to have your gains suddenly grind to a halt. A change, using six reps per set or whatever, could start a new growth cycle.

Quite a few Mr. Universe and Mr. Olympia winners (Samir Bannout, Arnold Schwarzenegger, Mohamed Makkawy, Sergio Oliva, Franco Columbu) actually practiced a system of relatively low reps during their early training. This seems to happen so often that it could be construed as recommended practice. Indeed, many champions give credit to early strength-training routines as forming an important basis of their physical achievements.

Perhaps low-rep training has a purpose for bodybuilders early in their careers. The evidence would seem to indicate it. However, there are numerous successful bodybuilders who never did much heavy power work. Steve Reeves is one. Larry Scott, Vince Gironda, Steve Davis Danny Padilla, Robby Robinson, Rick Wayne, Lou Ferrigno, Rocky DeFerro, Bill Grant, and many more . . . all developed prize-winning physiques *without* first doing heavy low-rep training.

Bill Pearl—now in his fifties, but still one of the best-built men of all time—made a habit of performing high *and* low reps in his training.

"In this way I get the best of both worlds," Pearl said. "There is definitely a different effect on the muscles between a system of high reps and one of low reps. So I use both when training for maximum results."

Vince Gironda (coauthor of *Unleashing the Wild Physique*, Sterling Publishing Co., Inc., NY) explains that there are certain muscle groups that require the use of high repetitions for maximum growth stimulation. The Iron Guru put it this way: "Calves and forearms, because of their large number of tightly packed muscle fibres in their respective areas, are considered *high-rep* muscles."

This is not to say that calves and forearms will not respond to lower reps. They probably will to some extent. But the information gleaned over the last hundred years has favored higher reps for these two areas.

Science has *not* come up with an ideal number of reps to perform in each exercise. What we have is better—the empirically gathered data of many years of experience. It may be true that sets of eight reps give us an honest workout, or that muscle fibre is best stressed by sets of five or six heavy reps, but there is always the possibility of attaining extra dimensions when we push the reps to twelve or even fifteen. As we approach this stage, we feel a "burn" in the muscles, and we confront the pain barrier.

It can be concluded that six to eight reps are ideal for pumping up the muscle fibres (muscle fibres can be individually enlarged, but are not capable, according to current scientific data, of increasing in number) and that eight to twelve repetitions per set (with more reps for some areas) are recommended for capillary and mitochondria growth (each can enlarge and multiply in number). Developing muscle is a two-way situation: (1) building muscle fibres by increasing resistance so that the muscles repair and overcompensate for future stress, and (2) developing more myofibrils, capillaries, mitochondria, and strengthening nerve pathways to feed the new growth.

You must incorporate *both* systems to maximize results. Many champion bodybuilders do this almost instinctively.

Look at the physique of a man or woman who is using a system of low reps (four or five)

Samir Bannout performs a cable curl.

exclusively. You can perceive a certain thickness to the muscles. Now check out the appearance of the high-rep trainer. The muscles pop out, have height, but the thickness is missing. Alternate performing low and high reps for the ultimate in cross-sectional thickness and muscle height. You'll look great!

# SHOCK TREATMENT

After a layoff from weight training, when you return to the weights your progress is rapid. You make fast gains. But after making substantial development, your growth will slow down and finally stop completely. You can push on with your routine, force the reps, add more weight, eat and rest more, but the out-

*Gladys Portugues works her biceps on a preacher bench.*

come is always the same: You're stuck! Your muscles just won't grow any larger.

Progressive-resistance exercise creates an ongoing *stress* by enlarging and strengthening the muscles, but they soon learn to adjust to a particular routine. Trainer Vince Gironda said, "Your muscles adjust to a new training regimen within five workouts."

Whatever the adjustment period, it is well known that merely repeating a workout is no guarantee that your growth cycle will proceed uninterrupted. New stresses, or shocks (changes), have to be found. You should, however, understand that sticking points are a natural part of the bodybuilding process. There is no such thing as continuous growth. In fact, the body needs slow periods to adjust and consolidate the effects of your training.

As an ambitious and serious bodybuilder, you should take steps to limit both the length and the frequency of sticking points. This is done by surprising your muscles with new techniques, routines, set-and-rep combinations, different frequency and intensity. In fact, you should do anything to stimulate your muscles into growth. With its numerous routines, principles, and new techniques, this entire volume could be claimed as being almost totally devoted to shock-training strategies.

The usual way to beat a sticking point is to surprise the muscle by "hitting" it from several different angles. This is known as a *blitz*. Mohamed Makkawy improved his back by applying this form of attack. He used three different back routines. His trainer, Vince Gironda, was right when he told Mohamed that this method would keep his muscles from getting too accustomed to a particular routine. Makkawy's back improved dramatically.

If your sticking point is the result of overwork, then a short layoff may be the answer. But do not make a habit of layoffs. A change is invariably more helpful than a rest. For the most part, a layoff sets *back* your training progress.

Arnold Schwarzenegger and Reg Park both overcame their lower-leg underdevelopment by throwing themselves into a very heavy, high-set program of standing calf raises on a daily basis. Both men used in excess of 800 pounds on the calf machine, and each was re-

Scott Wilson squeezes out one more rep on a machine.

warded with three additional inches of calf development, which had previously eluded them no matter how hard they trained.

I am convinced that many sticking points begin in the mind rather than in the muscles. Either boredom has set in, or enthusiasm has waned. If such is the case, then you need to revitalize your mental approach.

When I was training hard as a youngster in the 1960s in London, England, I was full of enthusiasm, pep, and ambition. Five or six of us at the small gym where we trained were able to bench press around 250 pounds, press behind neck about 130, and squat with 350. We loved training and would inspire each other in every workout. Enthusiasm was high. In our small way, we were progressing well, although at the time our gains had been fairly stagnant over the last six months. Then it happened. Reg Park, then indisputably possessing the world's greatest physique, trained at our club

for a full week (four workouts!). "Working in" with Reg in the various lifts was so inspiring that *all the poundages that we lifted increased in all the main exercises*, such was the influence from his presence. That single fact taught me something: *However hard you think you are training—however gung ho on your workouts, there is always a new plateau waiting to be reached if the mental motivation is strong and clear enough.*

As the memory of Reg Park's visit declined, so did the poundages that we had used when he was training alongside us. Fortunately, we didn't quite slip back to square one, but the immediate exhilaration of his visit had passed and so had our monumental gains, all achieved in the space of four workouts with Reg. Inspired motivation works like *magic*. You can float on air and reach out for the stars when you have it. To be without it is to place yourself in a mire of training stagnation.

*Mary Roberts*

# CHOICE OF EQUIPMENT

Today, more than ever before in history, we have an enormous availability of bodybuilding and fitness equipment. Each one supplies a means of activating your muscles. Invariably, this is achieved by offering different forms of weight-variable equipment—a resistance by which we can pit our current strength on a progressively more difficult basis.

The basic plate-loading barbell has still not been ousted from its number-one spot of popularity and effectiveness. Although there are machines which enable a person to isolate and train individual sections of muscle that free weights cannot duplicate, nevertheless, as tools for the job of toning muscles, increasing strength, and building mass, the lowly barbell (together with dumbbells and related free-weight machines) still remains at the top of the pile.

You probably have seen an advertisement for a product whereby a section of the ad relates a lot of "scientific data." Invariably, you are sent into dizzy confusion with Latin terminology, detailed microscopic illustrations, chemical formulas, and other obscure material. You are confused by the overly technical aspects, yet somehow authenticity is added to the promotion, and you are taken in by its claims.

The promotion of new bodybuilding machines is no different. The usual sales pitch is to first put down the barbell, depicting it as an antiquated, almost useless training device. Next you hear the reasons why a particular unit is ideal. The claims are endless. In fact, at least five equipment manufacturers claim to deliver the *fastest* results. Some people are clearly stretching the truth when you read this statement in five different companies' brochures.

Meanwhile, as the claims are tossed back and forth, the regular barbell, which doesn't

*Ed Guiliani does a barbell curl at the World Gym.*

belong to any single company, fails to get its fair share of credit. It is this writer's opinion that barbells and dumbbells are vastly superior to exercise machines when it comes to building muscle tone, mass, and strength in the fastest possible time. I am not alone. Every champion bodybuilder who has ever won a major contest—male or female, tall or short, young or not so young—has trained with barbells and dumbbells and related free-weight apparatus for most of their training time. And that includes the Mentzer brothers, Boyer Coe, and Casey Viator, all of whom have been publicized at one time or another as *machine devotees*.

It has been speculated that the more aggressive person would, if left to his or her own devices, prefer to use weights, while the unaggressive trainer would choose to work with machines. Women often get started on machines, because they frequently have a natural aversion to the use of weights. However, once they get into their training, weights invariably play an increasingly important role.

Take the regular squat exercise (a deep-knee bend with a loaded barbell held behind the neck). No one who associates with bodybuilders or goes to gyms can possibly deny that the squat is the king of all thigh builders. It has a greater effect on building leg mass and strength than any machine yet devised.

The bench press is supreme for developing the chest. Upper-body mass comes within a few short weeks when this exercise is performed regularly. No machine fully duplicates the effects.

The barbell curl is another free-weight gem. There doesn't exist a curl machine that gives equal or faster results.

But machines do have advantages. Their effects are worthwhile . . . as *adjuncts* to free-weight exercise. I've stated many times in print that one day the machine may indeed become the bodybuilder's most important piece of equipment. But it's not time to roll away the barbells yet! On the weightlifting scene today, free weights dominate when it comes to speedy results. The usefulness of machines is in their multi-angle applications. You can "hit" a certain part of a muscle with particular machines that you cannot easily exercise with free weights. There is no doubt that the hack machine, the various leg-press machines, and thigh-extension apparatus, enable the exerciser to work the legs from different angles.

In one of my previous books, *Beef It!* (Sterling Publishing Co., Inc., NY), I made a plea to inventors to get busy designing platforms and benches which will allow bodybuilders to continue to use the superior effectiveness of free weights, but in a greater variety of movements. We cannot change the one-directional resistance path of the barbell, because of gravity. But with ingenuity, we can change the body position in a thousand and one ways, to work the muscles from different angles with barbells and dumbbells.

*Chris Dickerson*

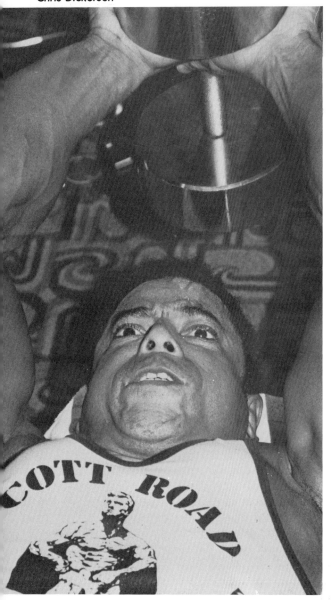

In the final analysis, remember that you are trying to get the most out of your training. You do not want to waste time. It is suggested, therefore, that you do not take sides in the issue over free weights or machines. Most gyms offer both free-weight equipment and a variety of high-tech apparatus. Don't get impressed by fancy chrome machines, and don't be fooled by the simple appearance of the disc-loading barbells and dumbbells. Be guided solely by the feel of how each affects your muscles. Become a thinking bodybuilder, and evaluate and decide for yourself. If things turn out as I predict, then you will opt for using free weights for 80 percent of your training, and about 20 percent with machines.

# CHANGING ROUTINES

It is possible to adapt to a new exercise or routine within three or four workouts. This book is full of routines, but why so many? The answer is that change is necessary. To perform the same exercise schedule week after week, month after month, invariably becomes counterproductive. If your mind doesn't lose its keenness to train, certainly your muscles will. Change is a necessary part of progress when it comes to any type of regimented exercise. You don't have to change your *whole* routine around. It's far better to just add an exercise or substitute a new movement for an older one that has temporarily lost its usefulness.

Of course, you can change your entire routine. The point to remember when you completely change routines, is to approach each new exercise with a degree of prudence. Don't go all out for the first few training sessions, if you are not used to the exercises involved. To do so is to invite injury, or at the very least, abnormally painful soreness the next day.

As mentioned earlier, the changing around of certain exercises is usually done to "shock" the muscles into renewed growth. But this is a tactic that has to be done with common sense. If you subject your muscles to *too* much shock treatment, you may upset your nervous system. This is one of the quickest ways to bring gains to a halt.

Let's assume that you have been doing four of five sets of squats each workout, but your thighs just don't show any improvement from one month to the next. So, having heard of "shock training," you decide that you are going to blitz those thighs to kingdom come, and instead of four or five sets, you are going to do ten sets. Make it an even dozen . . . more . . . fifteen sets!

Well, fifteen sets is going to shock your thighs all right. You'll find it difficult getting out of bed the next day! And what's more, you will be so sore and stiff that you probably won't be able to train your legs for a couple of weeks! But there's more. When you overtax your body, which is way over and beyond anything that you have attempted before, you upset your entire system. You may have a headache the next day, chronic diarrhea, or feel completely drained of energy.

By all means, change around some exercises, or perform a few extra sets to jostle your muscles into reacting—shock them—but don't traumatize them!

# INTENSITY CYCLING

Nature doesn't allow us to push our bodies to the limit *all* the time. Hence the coinage and relatively new usage of the word "peaking." We can only achieve our best condition momentarily. Muscles do not grow continually when we exercise. They make a sudden spurt in growth after progressive resistance has been applied, and then the growth slows or stops completely. There may even be a slight size and strength loss. If your workouts continue in

*Lee Haney*

a positive manner, your muscles will consolidate their previous gains, and if the progression factor is pushed hard enough, there will be another spurt in growth, again followed by a period of slow or non-existent progress. Each plateau of development must be fought for with mind and body.

This is what intensity cycling is all about. We have to accept nature's way of building muscle and take advantage of her laws. The mind must have a program for progress to

Brian Homka works his arms and shoulders to the max on a Nautilus machine.

reach new plateaus on a regular basis. It is not by coincidence that athletes from all over the world give their all-time best performances at the Olympic games. They prepare, plan, and strive for that peak period.

As a bodybuilder, you must also strive for results, not on an all-out continuous level, but on a cleverly planned basis of intensity cycling. As an off-season trainer, you should push hard to bring your body up in size. This training is the most productive of all. You are not in the final throes of contest preparation, which embraces the cutting-down process involving fewer calories, longer and faster workouts. You are building mass, thickness, and proportion—with the emphasis on *building*.

At this stage, many ardent bodybuilding enthusiasts simply go *all* out, *every* workout, in order to achieve their goals as quickly as possible. This is a mistake that will lead to injury or burn out—or both!

As bodybuilding writer Bill Reynolds said:

The best bodybuilders have learned to cycle the intensity level of their workouts from day to day, or week to week. On a four-day, off-season routine, you should train with 100 percent effort only once per week for each major muscle group, and just 90 percent of maximum the other times you train that body part.

Reynolds goes on to define 100 percent intensity in a set as going to failure and performing two or three forced reps beyond the point where another unassisted rep is impossible. Ninety percent intensity is going to the brink of failure, the last possible unassisted rep while still maintaining good exercise style. Of course, even this may be too exhausting for you. We all have different built-in tolerances for strenuous exercise.

# REST BETWEEN SETS?

For years, this question was answered dogmatically and clearly: *Repeat the next set of an exercise when your breathing has returned to normal.*

That same answer today has become oversimplistic. Because the physical stress you place on your muscles is intensified by the shortening of the time you take to complete that stress, rest periods are non-productive. *The shorter the better.* There are, however, other factors to consider. If you return to an exercise, such as the squat, before your breathing pattern has normalized, you will find that your cardiovascular system will be outrunning itself because of an accumulated oxygen debt. In other words, you will have to stop the set and return the weight to the racks before your thighs have been subjected to any growth-stimulating stress.

The single breath usually allocated to each repetition is barely enough to "feed" the system on heavy high-rep exercises such as bent-over rowing, squats, cleans, presses behind neck, deadlifts, and even bench presses and heavy curls. For this reason, you should not start a set of any of the above unless you have cleared up the oxygen debt from the previous set.

Lighter exercises can be resumed when there is a little breathlessness remaining; the important factor to bear in mind is that your conclusion of the set is due to muscular fatigue.

There is no doubt that during the preparation stage of bodybuilding competition, the aerobic effect of lessening the rest time between sets is conducive to enhanced cardiovascular endurance, greater caloric-burning function, and improved vascularity and definition.

Maintenance or off-season training involves moderately long rest periods of one to two minutes between sets (double that time for squats). It is important to keep the rest time between sets as even as possible. A loss of concentration, energy level, and even the pump itself will result if you rest one minute here, six minutes there, and so on. . . . The moral is clear. If you have to take a break, don't do it in the middle of working a particular area, and *never* in the middle of one specific exercise.

*Gladys Portugues clowns in front of the camera.*

# Part II

# THE WINNING EDGE

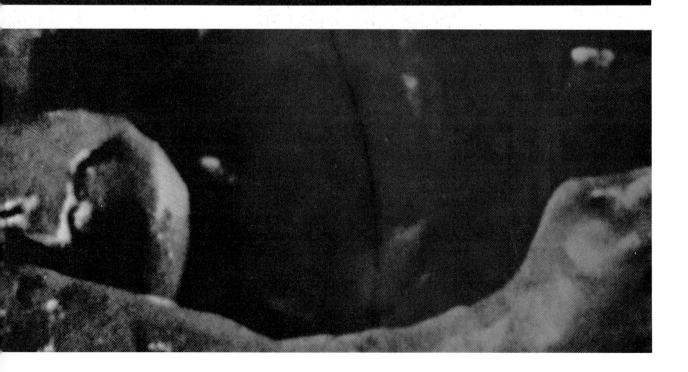

*Sergio Oliva*

**Y**our attitude in relation to the sport of bodybuilding is vitally important when it comes to developing the winning edge. Much of it may be fired from within until the results become evident. Those who lack this internal fire will have to drum up enthusiasm. A passive attitude about training, the lack of a forceful drive for achievement, can leave you in the middle of the gym with nowhere to go. You do not have the fight to improve nor the drive to go after superachievement.

Your attitude must be managed and shaped by control or cultivation, depending on whether you are overenthusiastic or undermotivated.

Overenthusiasm can lead to frustration and disappointment when fast results do not appear. If you are overenthusiastic, you are in the gym longer than is necessary. You work harder, not bad in itself, but invariably your training style is too "loose" for substantial progress. It can lead to acute anxiety and the eventual abandonment of all bodybuilding endeavors.

For those with a periodically negative attitude, the problem is different. There is no overenthusiasm to harness. Your job is to fight off negativity and develop drive, the vital compelling factor that will not rest until noticeable results have been obtained. Make every effort to cultivate the positive mental attitude that compels the necessary physical action in the gym. Get motivated!

This section looks at the ways in which you can take stock of yourself, set your priorities, and utilize practical steps towards attaining your bodybuilding goals.

*Bev Francis—the most massive female bodybuilder*

# GOAL SETTING

"It seems to me," said Harry Paschall in his famous book, *Muscle Moulding* (Iron Man Publishing Co.), "the first thing we should get out of the way in a physical improvement book, is why are you reading it? What do you want? What is your ultimate goal? Unless the objective is clear, you are not going to achieve full success."

Paschall was right on target about this vital bodybuilding concept. The most successful champions are those who have an almost photographically clear picture of what they wish to accomplish.

Physique champion Don Ross is a top-name bodybuilder who writes perceptively about the sport. In his book, *More Size, Power and Muscularity* (Iron Man Publishing Co.), he said:

> You will become what you *know* you will become. Most champs have one thing in common; they all *knew* they would do it! (Notice I said *would* and not *could*.) They pictured in their minds, time and time again, what they would accomplish.

Of course, the champion of positive self-image philosophy is Arnold Schwarzenegger. He came to America penniless (Joe Weider paid his way). Within a few years he was not only winning every contest around, but he was also very financially secure.

One effective way to set a goal for yourself is to pick a top bodybuilder whom you feel has a body structure similar to your own. Obviously, it would be a mistake to pick Arnold Schwarzenegger if you have narrow shoulders and wide hips, or Bev Francis if you were a small-framed woman.

If your role model fails to inspire you as time goes by, then get someone new to emulate and start developing along those lines. Years ago, from the turn of the century until the early 1920s, Eugene Sandow was a role model for half the civilized world—until it was revealed that he had flat feet, which was considered physically unacceptable in those days. Then came John Grimek in the 1940s, who could not only show the biggest muscles of his era, but also lifted phenomenal poundages and performed amazing gymnastic movements.

Steve Reeves, Hercules of the silver screen, became the idol of America's iron slingers in the 1950s. Then Reg Park, Sergio Oliva, Arnold Schwarzenegger, Lisa Lyon, Frank Zane, Lou Ferrigno, and Rachel McLish arrived on the bodybuilding scene. Each era has its superstars according to the fashion of the day.

John Grimek—a legend in the 1940s

Sergio Oliva—a modern-day Hercules

Goal setting must be a twofold activity. First of all, you should set an overall ideal idol in your mind. Whether he or she is a contemporary bodybuilding champion or one from the past is irrelevant. This is your long-term goal. Secondly, you should set short-term, *realistic* goals on a regular basis. Of course, do not set new goals until you have achieved the previous ones. Mr. Olympia Lee Haney once said:

Before you think about doing reps on the bench press with 400 pounds, you have to be able to rep out with 250, 300, and 350 pounds. Don't think about the NPC national title until you work at winning a city title, then state and regional competitions.

Once you have set a short-term goal, visualize it clearly and go after it with a firm commitment. You *will* achieve it.

As Joe Weider has said: "The notion of *trying* admits the possibility of failure. If you are convinced you'll achieve a goal, you don't say you'll try it; you just go ahead and do it!"

# GENETICS

Potential is something we can seldom be sure about. True, it will show itself after a few months, or maybe after a year of training, but you still may not *know* if you have the perfect genetics needed to build the perfect physique. Obvious "naturals" in the sport include Sergio Oliva, Lee Haney, Steve Reeves, Cory Everson, Bob Paris, and Gladys Portugues. The chances of your being among these elite are slim.

Arnold Schwarzenegger once said that potential is not just a physical characteristic:

> We have to split genetics into physical potential and mental potential. I was into soccer, skiing, powerlifting, swimming, and curling, but it wasn't until I got interested in bodybuilding that I felt my hidden mental potential positively unleash!

Physical potential is the ease at which your muscles grow, the shape and length of your bones, and the position of your muscle origins and insertions. Muscles are attached around the body according to the shape of the bones beneath them. A good skeleton is a great aid to the prospective bodybuilder. Both men and women do best in this sport if they have fairly wide shoulders, narrow hips, medium-sized bones, and an equally allocated degree of muscle cells in all areas (typified by muscles with long middle areas).

Often, however, an individual will have wide shoulders and narrow hips, yet not have a large amount of cells in the arms or legs. Conversely, many narrow-shouldered individuals have enormous potential for building huge arms and legs.

The mystery surrounding individual training requirements and differences in individual potential has been solved. The key is deoxyribonucleic acid—DNA—the genetic ingredient that determines our individual traits. It forms the basis of all life and "carries" the inherited traits from our forefathers to us. DNA is only partially understood at present.

Gladys Portugues is a bodybuilding natural.

Although everyone is capable of improving his or her physical state at any period with bodybuilding, it is harder for a person not genetically endowed as a "natural."

Genetic distribution includes the color of your eyes and hair, your basic intelligence, height, blood type, and so on. As far as bodybuilding is concerned, the important factors are:

## Somatotype

According to Dr. W. H. Sheldon, we all possess genetics that lean towards either *endomorphy* (round, heavy, big-boned types), *mesomorphy* (athletic, muscular, square-built types), or *ectomorphy* (slim, nervous, energetic, low-body-fat types). Obviously, those of us who lean towards the *mesomorphic* are best suited to bodybuilding.

## Physical Proportions

Balanced bone lengths and equally distributed muscle cells are important to all athletes.

## Fat Distribution

A low number of inherited adipose (fat) cells is ideal. People whose ancestry has originated in hot countries (as opposed to northern countries) often have the advantage of a low number of fat cells.

## Muscle Length

Long muscle attachments are helpful. Interestingly, an individual may have a long biceps and a high (or short) calf muscle, or a short biceps and a long calf. Muscle length is not uniform throughout the body.

## Frame Size

Bones should be large enough to support and enhance big muscles. *Overlarge* bones spoil the aesthetic appearance of "neat" joints, which are evident in the superior bodybuilder.

## Neurological Efficiency

High neurological performance enables an individual to contract maximum amounts of muscle fibres and therefore build muscle mass. This contractile capacity enables one to exert great amounts of intensity.

## Physiological Tolerance to Exercise

Basic, vigorous good health is an inherited trait that incorporates a high tolerance level for strenuous, regular bodybuilding exercises, and enables the body to repair (recuperate) itself quickly.

# STICKABILITY AND CONCENTRATION

Nothing can take the place of perseverance. Ability will not; many men who possess substantial natural abilities are failures. Intelligence alone is not the answer. Every one of us can immeasurably increase our powers and progress by adhering to a persistent path, first visualized, and then unswervingly maintained.

Simply *wishing* for a better body is not enough. It is an individual's stickability that gets the job done. When asked about his genius, Thomas Edison replied that it was 10 percent inspiration and 90 percent perspiration.

Do not miss workouts. If you feel like taking a layoff from training, then plan it methodically. Take a week off—two or three, if you wish—and then return to your training with a fresh enthusiasm, but do not fall into the trap of missing workouts. To do so is not conducive to achieving gains. It kills momentum. When you miss a workout there are many more bodybuilders who do not. And that puts them ahead of you in the rush for that trophy!

Of course, workout consistency is not of much use if there is no accompanying consistency of effort. There are many "gym regulars" who have been training for decades without making one iota of progress.

Stick to your resolve to come out of this sport a winner. Keep after your goal with relentless determination. To do this, you have to learn to concentrate. It is not something that comes to us naturally. Concentration means single-mindedness and it is not easy to apply 100 percent. Champions from the past—Vince

Gironda, Reg Park, and Clancy Ross—were said to be able to concentrate so thoroughly that a bomb could go off in the gym and they would hardly notice. Certainly none of these men would hear a telephone ringing while they were training, let alone answer it.

To merely concentrate on finishing the reps of a particular exercise is not enough. Your mind has to be focused on working out each specific muscle to the maximum.

For example, picture yourself doing wide-grip chins behind neck with a workout partner. You have both completed one set each of twelve reps. However, since this is a favorite exercise of his, he now hangs a 25-pound dumbbell from his belt and performs ten good repetitions. Your ego is ruffled. You *must* equal or better his performance. You take the dumbbell and start chinning. The first few reps go well and you start to feel it in your lats, then suddenly the next rep is hard. You are starting to fail. Determined to do ten reps, you now focus your mind on completing them. In order to accomplish this, your chinning style deteriorates into an all-out jerk pullup, instead of a smooth wide-grip, elbows-back, chin behind neck.

Even though you've completed the reps, you did it *without* working the lats, which is why you chose the movement in the first place. Granted you were concentrating, but the focus turned to the importance of completing the set instead of pumping the lats. You ended up doing a second-rate arm workout!

By all means, use heavy weights, really push for more, but never take your concentration away from the muscle you are working. Right now, consider whether you are using the misguided method in the previous example. If so, you will need to restructure your thinking about rep performance.

If your mind is cluttered with emotional problems, business worries, or school studies, you will have difficulty concentrating in your workouts. Try and leave your worries outside the gym or arrange your life in a way that excessive outside stresses are minimized.

Practice the fullest concentration when performing your exercises. Without it, you are wasting your time.

*Rachel McLish exercises her thighs on a leg-press machine.*

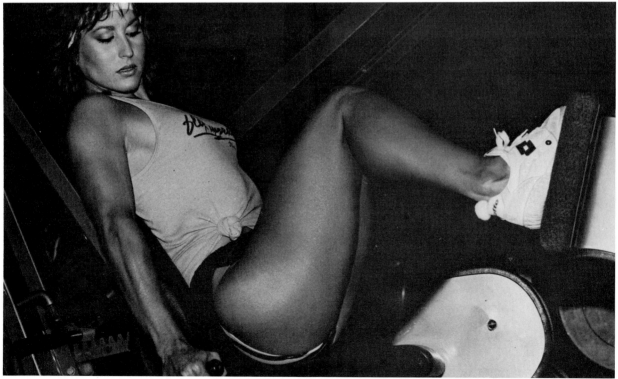

# STRETCHING

Years ago only ballerinas and field athletes stretched prior to performing their physical activities. A hardcore bodybuilder wouldn't even consider stretching before a workout. Today everyone—from Arnold Schwarzenegger and Tom Platz to Rachel McLish and Cory Everson—stretches.

There are some scientifically substantiated reasons why stretching before a workout actually helps to prevent injuries. It puts your muscles in tune with movement and prepares them for the ill effects of possible overextension of joints, muscles, or connective tissues. Statistically, 48 percent fewer overextension injuries occur in athletes and bodybuilders who have stretched a few minutes prior to their workouts.

Stretching also helps to enhance your natural posture, lengthens your muscles, and generally improves your appearance. There's also the personal satisfaction in being supple

Frank Zane

*A floor stretch is helpful for limbering up—Debbie Duncanson shows how.*

enough to do a full split or touch your head to your knees while your legs are locked. Additionally, regular stretching promotes both health and fitness and can relieve tension. It blends perfectly with a weight-training program, not just as a warm-up, but as a way of winding down from intense physical exertion. In fact, three-time Mr. Olympia Frank Zane, who conducts five-day seminars at his famous Palm Springs Zane Haven establishment, actually recommends stretching *between* exercises.

Finally, stretching has a particular use for the competitive bodybuilder. It enables the individual to execute difficult poses more easily. The more flexible the performer becomes, the greater the psychological and physiological edge in actual competition.

You should stretch several times a week, before and after your workouts and, if possible, at particular times during the day, even on off-training days.

When stretching, do not allow enthusiasm to get the better of you. Never bounce excessively, nor strive to overachieve. Stretching is a slow, studied procedure. It is gentle in nature. Watch your cat or dog when it awakes. Note that prolonged, easygoing stretch, which eases the animal into movement.

When you stretch take a full minute to get into position of fullest extension. Stretch to the limit and then hold it for a few more seconds. Never push past the barrier of mild discomfort because this is a sure indication that you are tearing small muscle fibres. As with your bodybuilding exercises, stretching can be performed in sets and the actual position can be held for progressively longer periods, up to two minutes each. Beginners should average ten minutes daily at their stretching whereas the more advanced trainers could devote up to 20 minutes or more each day to this important warm-up to exercise. Do the following five stretches before every workout.

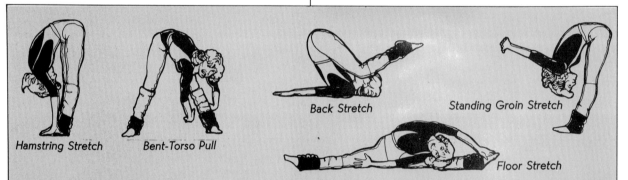

Hamstring Stretch      Bent-Torso Pull      Back Stretch      Standing Groin Stretch      Floor Stretch

## Hamstring Stretch

Lean your body forward as depicted. Do it slowly, with no bouncing. Hold the position for approximately 30 seconds, allowing your body weight to stretch the hamstring muscles (the backs of your legs). You will feel some mild discomfort at first. As you get used to this stretch, increase the tension slightly. Progressively lean over at a greater angle.

## Bent-Torso Pull

Lean over to one side and bend the upper body down until your chest touches your thigh, using your arms. Keep your feet spread at least a yard apart, and twist the waist towards the direction that you are stretching without bending at the knee. Work each side ten times and hold for about ten seconds each stretch. This is an excellent movement for flexibility for the entire back, hamstrings, and calves.

## Floor Stretch

Spread your legs apart to the sides as far as you can. Working one leg at a time, bend one knee while keeping the other leg straight with your head down. Try to bring your chest down to your thigh with the use of the arms. Hold the stretch for ten seconds. Do eight stretches to each leg.

## Standing Groin Stretch

Standing with feet a yard apart, try to touch your head to your knee. Remember, no bouncing! Just slowly bend the body down until your head is as close to your knee as possible and hold for ten seconds. Do the exercise six times for each side.

## Back Stretch

Lie on the floor on your back. Roll up on your shoulders, supporting the body with upper arms on the ground. Gradually and under control, lower your legs behind your head. Try to touch the knees to the floor by the sides of your head. Hold for 10–20 seconds, or longer when you get used to the position. This is very good for maintaining a limber spine, and you need only perform it once.

# OVERTRAINING SYNDROME

If you do not allow yourself enough time between workouts for your muscles to recuperate, then you will experience chronic fatigue. And as you can imagine, an overtrained situation occurs as the workouts pile up, and the body has not been allowed time to recover 100 percent from the previous session. It boils down to this: If you don't train hard enough, you won't improve. If you train too hard, you'll break down.

The more you train, the more careful you have to be to not step over that razor's edge into the overtraining syndrome. Armand Tanny, a former Mr. U.S.A., now in his sixties, is very opinionated about the modern training philosophies:

The expression *No Pain, No Gain*, runs rampant in training circles today. Innocently conceived, it has turned into an insidious standard, interpreted by most coaches and athletes to mean that muscle function will improve only when stimulated by work overload on every set of weight-training exercises. This interpretation is wrong and contradicts the reality of normal neuromuscular function.

There is benefit in continuing a set to exhaustion on an irregular basis, or for a limited number of sets, but when many sets of the same exercise are performed to exhaustion, the effect can be devastating. Most bodybuilders find that they can't overload a muscle group more than once a week without slowly pushing themselves into an overtrained state. Muscle tissue needs time to cleanse itself of lactic acid and other overload by-products. Attempting to work a muscle before it has fully recuperated will lead to a systematic breakdown, mental apathy, and even injury.

Whereas most experienced bodybuilders can *feel* when they are overtraining (and take steps to either lessen the intensity or frequency of their workouts), many find that the symptoms are not obvious, and that they creep up gradually, choking off progress without the trainer being aware of the true problem.

Joseph A. Miller, the strength and conditioning coach of the National Hockey League and who is affiliated with the President's Council on Physical Fitness and Sports in Washington, D.C., has designed a simple daily test to help avoid overtraining. Since heart rate (pulse) is related to the amount of catecholamine in the blood, the stress hormone released when we put our bodies through too many sets of forced reps, by simply monitoring our heart rate on a regular basis we can observe whether or not an impending state of overtraining and physical breakdown exists. In other words, if your heart rate at rest is over and above that which is normal for you, you're on the verge of the overtraining syndrome.

Miller offers a viable safeguard to avoid this syndrome:

Follow this simple procedure. Upon awakening in the morning, lie still in bed for five minutes, then record your resting heart rate. Following that, rise, routinely weigh yourself and record a second resting pulse count. After your day's weight-training session, again record your body weight and resting heart rate. These recordings should be taken only after you have showered and rested in a reclining position for 15 minutes.

The next day repeat the entire sequence, beginning with the morning recording and following with the after-workout analysis.

How do you use these numbers? Plotted over a period of 7–28 days, the morning heart rate will provide key information about the possibility of overtraining. If there are increases over this period, it is evidence that you are overstressing the system. If you see such a steady or sudden rise in your morning readings, you must immediately *decrease* both the volume and intensity of your training efforts. If this is done in time, you should be able to avoid overtraining completely.

The second heart rate, or that which you record after your workout, also has great value, for it will tell you whether you have trained too intensively. If this heart rate (taken 15 minutes after finishing the workout) is elevated more than five beats above that taken in the morning, you may have overextended yourself in this particular training session. If so, you should structure your next workout to be less stressful (with a slower pace, less volume, less weight, or less intensity of effort).

The overtraining syndrome is more common today than ever. Every bodybuilder has fallen into its trap at some time or other. Overtraining leads not only to staleness, depression, an irritability, but also to weight loss, chronic fatigue, and worse—your muscles take on an unimpressive flat, stringy appearance.

# RELAXATION AND SLEEP

These two aspects relate very strongly to the overtraining syndrome. Muscle recuperates during rest and sleep. This is the *only* time it grows. You must have sufficient rest time and sleep to allow your muscles to recover.

Over 30 years ago, editor of *Vigor* magazine John Barrs wrote:

It is very difficult to overwork the *muscles* of a bodybuilder, but very easy indeed to drive the nervous system too hard. Clinical and laboratory experiments have indicated that the muscles themselves can withstand phenomenal demands. But when a weight trainer continues an exercise until he simply cannot perform another repetition it is the nervous mechanism rather than the muscle fibres which is unable to cope.

According to physiologists, the first to fatigue in the neuromuscular system are the motor cells in the brain; the nerve "end plates"

are the next elements to exhaust and *then* the muscle fibres; the nerve itself is almost impossible to exhaust. Forcing oneself with exercise past reasonable fatigue—to exhaustion—expends a lot of nervous energy. This accounts for Mike Mentzer's extremely intensive, yet relatively short workouts.

*Andre Maille*

Carolyn Cheshire

or eight hours, and a few bodybuilders are not ashamed to admit that they like to get as much as ten hours of sleep nightly.

A bodybuilder, keen to add muscle mass, would be wise to limit physical activities other than training. You cannot reasonably expect to gain muscle size if you run several miles after your workouts and go out on the dance floor after that. You only have so much available energy. If you overextend yourself, you will kill off your chances of progressing. Even a physically demanding job such as manual labor or farming may hold some people back, especially those with already high metabolic rates.

Avoid playing extra sports while trying to increase muscle mass. Later, when you have acquired your muscles, you can return to fun and games.

Do not turn your hard training into wasted effort by ignoring the importance of obtaining sufficient rest, relaxation, and sleep.

# TRAINING PARTNERS

Since benches and squat racks have barbell holders, it could be argued that training partners are not really necessary. Certainly, not all bodybuilders use them. Nevertheless, a pattern does seem to materialize as competition time comes around. Training partners become more evident. Of course, forced reps always require at least one training partner. It can't be any other way. Casey Viator said:

A certain type of personality in a training partner helps me train to the maximum. If I end up with a real flake, I don't get anything out of it. I have to have partners who are very reliable and dedicated, who won't miss any workouts, and who can consistently push me past my limits.

When you use a training partner you must have someone who has your interest at heart;

The reason why most experts advocate the use of split routines, or alternatively less frequent training, is not so much to provide rest periods for the muscles but to allow the nervous system to recover from fatigue.

Progressive bodybuilders should try to relax completely at times during the day, putting their feet up, if possible, for 20 minutes after meals. A midday nap can help competitive bodybuilders when they are in the throes of heavy training. The amount of sleep you need at night is an individual matter, but few people can get along with heavy training on much less than six hours each night. Most prefer seven

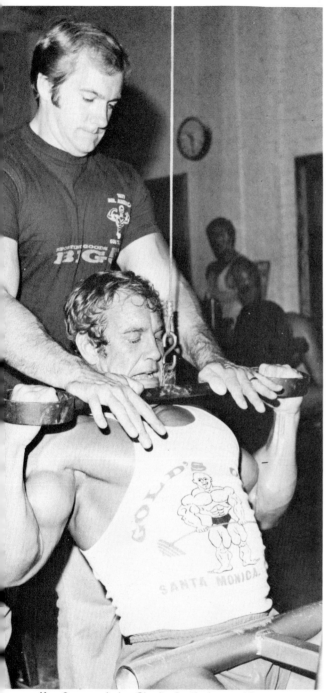

Ken Sprague helps Charlie Smith do a pulldown exercise.

know that all the noise is to attract attention to him or her, *not* to help you with doing the reps. On the other hand, a quietly spoken phrase, "come on, one more," as you conclude a set can be all that is needed to help you to victory.

Training partners are most useful—some say essential—in exercises like squats and bench presses, and many bodybuilders only have partners for these two exercises. Others, who enjoy the extra benefit of having someone in attendance while they train, will use a training partner for all exercises.

There is a trend today for bodybuilders to work out with members of the opposite sex. Apparently the desire to "show off" is more pronounced when you train with someone of the opposite gender. Hormone release can be greater, training effort increased, and resulting gains more noticeable.

Finally, when you know that your training partner is waiting for you at the gym, you will not find it so easy to miss workouts. Since consistency in training is one great key to success, a training partner can provide a really big incentive.

Gladys Portugues gets a lift from Mohamed Makkawy as she does a wide-grip pullup to chest.

likewise you must show return respect and interest to help with their training. You can tell if your workout partner is tuned in to what you are doing. If you notice that your partner is shouting and screaming at you to complete a set *before* the reps are getting diffcult, you

# BREATHING PATTERNS

I would say that half the bodybuilding books available today advocate that the trainer slowly breathe in and out through the nose. The writer invariably goes on to warn: "Never hold your breath!" Are they correct? No. Neither are the so-called authorities who say: "Don't think about breathing—it will happen naturally." Well, I'm the first to admit that breathing will take place whether we think about it or not, but like the exercises themselves, breathing has to be thought about, controlled, and managed. You cannot rely on your lungs to make the right demands.

Breathing can, and often does, vary from one exercise to another, but as a guideline you should breathe in quickly through the mouth just prior to the hardest part of an exercise.

*T-bar rowing . . .*
*Scott Wilson-style*

*Kevin Lawrence and Diana Dennis*

Just as quickly, the air should be expelled through pursed lips as the hardest part of an exercise is completed. It is almost impossible to do a high-intensity repetition *without* holding your breath.

As far as breathing through the nose is concerned, this is just not possible during vigorous exercise like weight training. The nasal passages are not set up for huge rushes of air. Always breathe through the mouth during a demanding exercise.

Another aspect of breathing while training is the air you take in *between* sets. Listen to the Iron Guru Vince Gironda, coauthor of *Unleashing the Wild Physique* (Sterling Publishing Co., Inc., NY):

> If you are training with good tempo, don't just allow your body to recover between sets by sitting down and panting. Load up with oxygen. Hyperventilate. Place your hands on your thighs (knees bent) and lift

Mike Christian

your chest high as you slowly take each breath through pursed lips. After taking five or ten breaths in this manner, you should be ready to begin your next set. I call this "oxygen loading."

It's not hard to see how the muscles benefit from Vince's oxygen-loading principle. By forcing oxygen into the system (through the lungs), you are speeding up repayment of the oxygen debt created by your last set of exercise. Among other things, you get a terrific pump.

You will find that some movements require two or even three breaths per repetition, while other exercises are so undemanding on the cardiovascular system that you may only require to breathe every second or third rep. For the most part, however, the best way to take in air during your training is to breathe once every repetition. This has the added benefit of pacing your reps and helping the rhythm of your exercise in general.

# RECORD KEEPING

Frank Zane, three-time Mr. Olympia, is known to have kept a training diary for the last 20 years. (Actually, he's been training with weights for over a quarter of a century.) Why is keeping a journal so valuable? He said:

> I can check my day-to-day progress. It gives me something to beat, and with a flick of the pages I can see what I was doing last year at this time and know whether I am ahead or behind schedule.

Frank loves to physically peak every September, whether he chooses to enter the IFBB Mr. Olympia contest or not. He starts into serious workouts each spring and follows a three-phase cycle-training program until he peaks out his physique in the early fall. The

Frank Zane has kept a training diary for the last 20 years.

If you are taking a protein or vitamin supplement, keep a record of it. Then you are in a position of being able to check the variables involved in your progress. Your measurements should be recorded at least every month, more frequently if your gains are rapid. You may not be able to record your exact fat percentage, but caliper readings at the side of the waist, mid-thigh, and at the triceps are very useful indicators.

Even your short- and long-range goals can be itemized in your training log. When you get to the 19-inch-arm stage you may get a smile from looking back in your training diary and noting an early reference to "achieve 14-inch arms by end of year."

If you want to enjoy a little unrecorded training for a few months, then by all means forget the record book for a while. It'll take the pressure off and your workouts may be

John Hnatyschak

idea behind Zane's method is to gradually increase the intensity of his training during the spring and summer.

A training diary helps you to keep on top of your workouts. It sharpens your attention to what's happening. What should you record in your training diary? Everything that could be pertinent to your training. Sets, reps and poundages used, together with your body weight, must be recorded. But you should also make notes on the training style used; whether a particular set was excessively difficult. Each day's entry must be dated, and note the time of day at which you trained.

When you achieve a new record in an exercise put an asterisk beside the set in question. A record can be merely the performance of more reps in an exercise. You do not have to add 20 pounds to the bar in order to qualify for a record. You can also list your food intake (the overall daily calorie consumption, if you are so inclined), and in this way you will be able to look back and see how your eating habits influence both your weight and strength.

more enjoyable, but at times when you want to really push to a new plateau, you simply must use the advantages offered by keeping a training log. You put more pressure on yourself, but that is what makes you succeed.

# INJURIES

Weight training is really a very safe sport, especially when compared to the hazards that can occur in football, soccer, boxing, and hockey, just to mention a few.

*Always warm up with at least one set of high repetitions in every exercise you do. Do not use too light a weight or no effect will be felt.
*Work the muscles equally. If you are doing heavy squats, always do heavy leg curls. If you work your side deltoids hard, give equal attention to your front and rear deltoids Work your back as hard as your abdominals. A chain is as strong as its weakest link. Sooner or later the weak one will snap.
*Stretch your limbs and back regularly. Never involve your muscles in bouncing movements in the squat or deadlift. Do not even stretch using bouncing movements.
*Never attempt a maximum weight if you haven't been practicing low reps in your training. Do not let your pride push you into a

*Bill Denk puts everything into a dumbbell press.*

"Injury is another name for error," said Armand Tanny. It's true, for with care a bodybuilder can avoid serious injury if a little common sense is used. In spite of this fact, most trainers manage to hurt themselves sooner or later, and even if the injuries themselves are not life threatening, they can cause a bodybuilder to lose a great deal of training time. Here are a few pointers to *prevent* injury:

situation using a heavy weight on an exercise you are not currently practicing. Take no dares or bets regarding heavy lifts.
*Do not deviate from using good style during heavy training. Lower the bar to the same part of your chest when doing bench presses. Squat with the normal foot position. Row, curl, chin, and press in the way your body knows best and practices most often. If you

make a change, begin with light resistance.
*Eccentric contractions (lowering the weights) cause severe levels of muscle soreness and can, if taken to extremes, cause muscle strains and tears.

When an injury occurs it will usually show itself as a sharp pain. Sometimes this is only a mild twinge, and at other times it is so sudden and concentrated that you will collapse to the ground. If you notice a strange "twitch" in your shoulder or back while exercising, stop. Do not perform that movement for several weeks. If you continue, a full-fledged muscle tear could result. When this happens apply ice to the area immediately and rest up to three weeks or even more, if necessary.

Never force yourself to train using an exercise that causes excessive pain. Sooner of later you will rip the muscle area seriously. You can train *around* an injury. Use an exercise for the same body part, but one that does *not* cause any discomfort. Occasionally, you will not be able to do any exercise for an injured body part. When this happens you have to be content with working only surrounding muscles. You will keep some size and the injury will heal faster because the surrounding activity brings blood to the area in force.

Not all injuries are muscle tears. Tendinitis and bursitis and lower-back pain are other real possibilities. The most common is tendinitis, the tendon inflammation of the elbows and the knees. Bursitis is the inflammation of a bursa (a cavity usually containing fluid that reduces friction, as between a tendon and bone).

Exercises that often cause elbow pain are triceps pulley pressdowns, lying triceps curls, and single-arm dumbbell stretches. Tennis players can get it, as can house painters, golfers, and window cleaners.

Knee problems can come from hack lifts, sissy squats, or any leg movement which puts the knee joint at a huge disadvantage. Multi-joint movements are safer on your elbows and knees than isolation movements. Squats are better than thigh extensions. Close-grip bench presses are better than triceps curls. Dumbbell presses are safer than dumbbell laterals. Bench pressing is a less hazardous movement than straight-arm flyes, and barbell curls are safer than preacher curls.

*Mohamed Makkawy*

When it comes to lower backs, we all hurt this area to a greater or lesser degree at one time or another. The best single exercise for injury-free progress is the hyperextension. No *downward* pressure is brought into play as is the case with deadlifts, good-morning exercises, squats, and rows.

Hyperextensions are performed by extending off the edge of a bench face down, with the legs pinned down across the bench. The upper body moves in a 90-degree arc from an L-shape (head near floor) position to a straight-out horizontal position. There is no direct pressure on the vertebrae, as is the case with standing exercises.

It is an unfortunate fact that all athletes—bodybuilders included—push their training towards an occasional injury. Lou Ferrigno said: "Injury is an inherent part of training. Prevention and treatment should have high priority. Be aware and attentive and enjoy a full life in the sport."

# NUTRITION AND SUPPLEMENTS

There are no secret foods or food combinations that will give you fantastic muscle gains. Nutrition for the bodybuilder is ideally about the same as for anyone else interested in health and fitness, with one difference: Slightly larger amounts of protein are required to accommodate muscle growth.

Do not make junk foods a regular part of your food intake. There will be occasions when you have no choice, but keep junk food consumption to a minimum. Junk foods are high-calorie, sugar-loaded goodies that have little nutritional value. You see them in abundance on the shelves of convenience stores. They last for months because they are loaded with chemical preservatives to keep them from going bad. There's virtually no goodness in these foods, only useless calories which will cause you to gain fat. People who eat this kind of food have an unhealthy look about them. Look at their lack of skin tone and blotchy faces. Their eyes lack the sparkle of health, and their hair is lacklustre. Sometimes cellulite is apparent.

Contrast this unhealthy appearance with the person who eats wholesome, high-fibre natural foods that contain no chemical additives. The difference is amazing.

Vince Gironda believes in the importance of *stone-age nutrition*. He contends that since the early days of man, the quality of our diet has only regressed. It's true that the average diet today is appalling when dissected for wholesomeness and nutritional benefit. On the other hand, because of world trade today, those who desire to eat well can do so. There is a huge variety of food available to us today, more than ever before in the history of mankind.

Here is a list of some foods to avoid whenever possible: white, devitalized bread, candies, cakes, cookies, chocolate bars, table

*Jusup Wilkosz refuels with orange juice between sets.*

sugar, table salt, pies, doughnuts, puddings, pizza, spaghetti, hot dogs, smoked and processed meats, artificially colored meats, potato chips, beer, pretzels, ice cream, soft drinks, jams, salad dressings, sugar-loaded breakfast cereals.

You may be wondering just what you should eat! We should eat foods as closely as possible to the way nature presents them. I listed the worst, now for the best: whole-grain cereals and breads (especially if there is no added sugar or sodium), natural vegetables (steamed or raw), liver, poultry, fish, fruits, eggs, nuts, and yogurt.

Never fry meat, fish, vegetables, potatoes, or eggs. Do not remove edible peels from fruits and vegetables (but wash them thoroughly since they may have been sprayed with insecticides, etc). Add lemon juice to a salad rather than a regular dressing. Don't add salt or sugar to your food. Nature has already provided enough in fruits and vegetables. Instead, add natural herbs and spices. An apple is better than apple juice, an orange is better than orange juice. You need the fibre.

According to *Prevention* magazine, which promotes good health through sensible living, exercise, and optimal nutrition, the most advantageous foods to eat for super nutrition are as follows:

*Bananas*: High in potassium, vitamin $B_6$, and biotin.
*Bran*: Corn bran and oat bran are slightly superior to wheat bran.
*Beans*: High in magnesium and B vitamins, thiamine, and riboflavin.
*Cabbage* (including broccoli, brussels sprouts, cauliflower): All have been shown to contain anti-cancer-causing substances to "trap" carcinogens before they do damage to the body. High in potassium, vitamin A, calcium, and vitamin C.
*Carrots*: High in betacarotene and fibre, low in calories.
*Citrus Fruits*: High in vitamins C, A, and E, and pectin fibre. Helps to build muscle cells.
*Fish*: Good bodybuilding food, usually low in fat.
*Garlic and Onions*: May inhibit tumor growth and slow down blood-clot development.

*Couples champions Tina Plakinger and Tony Pearson*

*Kale* (spinach and leafy greens): Contains chlorophyll, vitamin A, calcium. Helps bone development.

*Liver*: Beef liver contains almost every nutrient known. Rich in iron, zinc, copper, choline, and inositol, as well as fat emulsifiers, vitamins A, E, K, thiamine, riboflavin, biotin and folic acid.

*Melons*: Low calorie, high in vitamin C.

*Nuts*: High calorie, excellent source of zinc (especially cashews and almonds).

*Oysters*: High in zinc (for cell growth) and good for proper prostate and sexual functions. Also rich in calcium, iron, copper, and iodine.

*Peppers*: Very high in vitamin C (for cell bonding).

*Poultry*: (turkey and chicken): Low in calories, high in essential nutrients, yet low in fat, especially if skin is removed.

*Seeds*: High in zinc and cell-building protein.

*Soybeans*: High in vegetable protein. Tofu and miso are soybean products.

*Sweet Potatoes*: High in vitamin A and natural fibre.

*Wheat Germ*: High in vitamin B, thiamine, and vitamin $B_6$.

*Whole-grain Products*: Whether for breads, cereals or rice, whole-grain products are superior because of their high-fibre qualities.

*Yogurt*: Rich in calcium and all nutrients. Can often be digested by those who have an intolerance to milk.

Good nutrition is balanced nutrition. You should include food from each of the following every day:

*Milk (milk, yogurt, cottage cheese, hard cheese)
*Meat (beef, veal, lamb, fish, poultry, eggs)
*Vegetables (fruits, vegetables, legumes, nuts)
*Grains (bread, cereals, rice)
*Fats (butter, margarine, oils)

The last group, fats, should be consumed in very small quantities.

For the bodybuilder, protein is an important ingredient, which is still the only substance that feeds and builds muscles. The name *protein* is derived from the Greek word *proteios*, meaning of primary importance. It is vital for successful bodybuilding. Without sufficient quantities, no gains will materialize.

British bodybuilding nutritionist Bernard Beverley said:

> Of the three major elements in your diet— carbohydrate, fat, and protein—protein is the most important because it is the only thing from which your body can recreate cells and stimulate growth. The two other items are primarily needed for energy. Protein is the constructor of the body.

When you exercise, the muscle cells are broken down and it is the ingested protein that enables them to build up during rest. What some bodybuilders fail to realize is that protein is required for many vital bodily functions, including the production of blood and hormones. Your teeth, bones, and even your hair need protein. You can be sure of one thing. The protein you eat will be utilized for body maintenance before any is allocated to increasing muscle hypertrophy.

Bernard Beverley wrote:

> A bodybuilder needs ample amounts of protein over and above the survival level. In relative terms, this means 0.6 grams of protein for every pound of body weight. So a 150-pound man would need 90 grams of protein daily. While the body will grow to some extent on this amount, by a strange quirk of nature, it is far easier for the system to absorb what it needs from an abundance rather than from just enough.

In other words, if you take in more protein than you need, you'll absorb what you do need much easier. A hard-training bodybuilder would probably require about one gram per pound of body weight to significantly increase muscle mass. Best protein foods include eggs, milk, organ meats (liver is excellent), red meats, poultry, fish, cheese, nuts. If you want to count up grams, most bookstores have calorie charts and gram-counter booklets, which sell for very modest cost.

A bodybuilder should always eat carbohydrates whenever he eats protein. If you do not have complex carbohydrates (vegetables, breads, cereals, rice, fruit) present with your protein, your system will convert the protein not into amino acids as it should for muscle building, but into urea, which is eliminated in your urine. You do not need great amounts of complex carbohydrates, but some are required each time you consume a high-protein food.

The question of what supplements to take is on every serious bodybuilder's mind. I suggest that you take a multi-vitamin/mineral pill regularly. Other worthwhile supplements include desiccated liver tablets, amino acids, and protein-powder supplements. Since the egg is the most biologically perfect protein food for bodybuilders (it is 95 percent biologically identical to human tissue), this would be the best protein powder to take. Milk is second in quality. Two of the most popular protein powders are Joe Weider's Milk and Egg and MuscleMag's Milk 'n Egg, but there are other good brands available.

I am aware of those who advocate excessive supplementation of individual vitamins in high dosages. Some people, not just bodybuilders, take 1000-milligram tabs of vitamin C, large amounts of B and E. (Toxicity can result from too much of vitamins A and D, so these are seldom taken in large doses.)

I do not believe that this type of excessive supplementation is necessary or even beneficial if indulged in all the time. Never forget that optimal health can be achieved by people who eat balanced meals. Supplementation is not in nature's original design. It is modern society's brainchild, to be used periodically to help achieve certain specific results.

*Bodybuilding writer Denie Walter (left) and Rick Wayne (center) enjoy the company of Joe Weider, "Trainer of the Champions."*

# Part III

# THE METHODS OF REPS

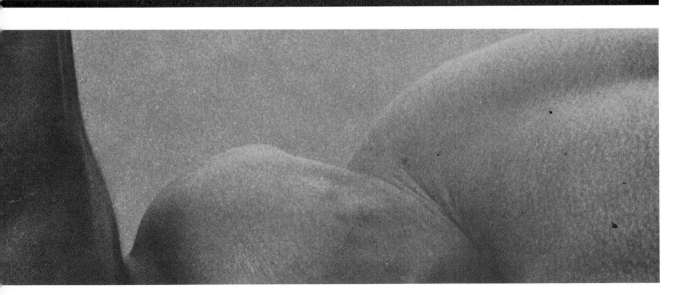

Arnold Schwarzenegger

The basic building block of every bodybuilder's routine is the rep—the single full-range movement of an exercise. It's not simply a matter of pressing a barbell over your head or casually curling a dumbbell. There are many ways to perform a single rep, and each produces a different effect on the various muscles.

From strict reps to cheat reps to slo-mo reps to negative reps, and other training-related techniques for building up your body, you'll find everything you need to know about how to perform a rep.

# STRICT REPS

The truly aggressive bodybuilder *rarely* performs strict repetitions. The very thought of this type of training runs contrary to his or her personality and demanding physical needs. Strict training, as explained earlier, is the lifting of a weight in a very smooth fashion, with no extraneous body motion.

For an ultrastrict curl, you would raise the barbell from the arms-straight-down position at the thighs to the completion of the exercise below the neck with no back bending, no forward leaning, and no knee bending. Only the forearms should move. The upper arms should stay tight in against the sides of the body. Very few trainers perform their curls in this way.

Strict exercises do have their place in the bodybuilder's schedule. I often think that all beginners should start off their first few months of training, using perfectly strict exercise form. In this way they will be more aware of perfect style, and they will instantly recognize any variations.

Strict training has the advantage of working the muscle from a prestretched, fully extended position. Obviously, this allows for a fuller contraction than if you started from something less than the extended position. The fullest contraction will occur only when the bar has travelled to the point where no more movement is possible. This is an absolute requirement for achieving the high-intensity muscular involvement necessary for fibre enlargement.

However, there are provisos for strict rep performance: the exercise must be completed without the help of momentum. You should

Dumbbell flyes for chest development as performed by Serge Nubret

When you perform strict repetitions you use perfect exercise style throughout the entire range of motion. Many bodybuilders are under the impression, at least by the way in which they exercise, that the only object in training is to merely get the weight from point A (the fully extended start position) to point B (the fully contracted finish position). This is a totally erroneous conception. The idea is not to travel between the points of extension and contraction in a stressless journey on the muscle involved, but just the opposite—to stress it to the hilt, and then some. If you don't *feel* a muscle working, then you cannot expect growth.

not rush your repetitions when trying to achieve maximum overload. Momentum carries the weight through the range of movement with the *least* involvement of the muscles. It is counterproductive to what you are trying to achieve from strict training.

You must work out with substantial resistance to involve a maximum number of muscle fibres. It is difficult to recruit *new* muscle-fibre action (which is the essence of overload training) without maximum effort and heavy weights for the style of performance used.

At the end of this section you will read about other methods that may seemingly contradict the usefulness of strict repetitions.

Each method should be adhered to at *different* times. Listen to your body. It will let you know when to embark on a cheating program, a power schedule, etc. Each brings something to a routine that the others cannot. Strict reps are an important part of your overall training procedure.

# CHEAT REPS

The word "cheating" as applied to bodybuilding is not an accurate description. It implies that you are doing something very wrong when, in reality, many so-called cheating movements are beneficial to the bodybuilder. In some cases, you cannot "hit" a particular muscle area *without* cheating.

Armand Tanny pointed out something in *Muscle & Fitness* magazine that is very educational with regard to the cheating principle. Using the lateral raise exercise as an example, he explained that the lateral deltoid heads are not really brought into play until the arms are well out, away from the sides of the body. These muscles continue to contract until the arms are at a 45-degree angle from the body.

Tanny explained:

> In order to perform a conventionally strict lateral raise, you have to use fairly light dumbbells. The stress on the main shoulder area is negligible, so how can you use a weight heavy enough to fully work the deltoid muscle? You can't change weights in the middle of the movement.

The cheating method of using loose style offers the only solution. If you bend the elbows, lean forward, and heave slightly, you can jettison the dumbbells upwards to engage the deltoids in the fullest possible involvement. Thus, they get the benefit of the heavier weight. This same technique can be applied to the barbell curl. The belly of the biceps is stimulated more when the bar is raised with some help from body motion. This is not to say that superstrict reps have no value. They do—start-

*Robby Robinson and Susan Roberts*

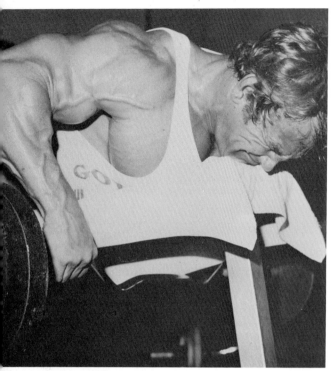

Charlie Smith

ing a barbell curl from a straight-arm position, with no body motion at all, benefits the lower part of the biceps.

Vince Gironda calls it "creative cheating." The idea is to use the method to beat a certain problem. Do not cheat for the sake of merely using heavier weights. Cheat to *achieve* a particular result. Just about every muscle area has a weak link. The cheating principle, if used correctly, can put the stress on an area of a muscle that usually doesn't work very much.

Cheating allows you to use heavier loads on the muscle areas that need heavier stimulation. You may choose to cheat during a set, from beginning to end, or else merely start cheating reps during the latter part of a set. Some even go so far as to cheat a weight up, only to resist its downward path vigorously. If you choose this method, make sure that your muscles are warmed up well.

Many bodybuilders claim they *only* use strict style in their training. In 30 years of observing beginners, intermediates, and professional world champions, I have never known a bodybuilder who didn't, at least occasionally, use the cheating principle.

# CUMULATIVE REPS

This is not a widely used technique. It works this way. Select a weight for an exercise that you can just about do ten reps with. Then perform one repetition with that weight in your selected exercise. Replace the weight on a bench or rack, count ten seconds, and then repeat the movement for two repetitions. Take another ten-second rest. Then perform three repetitions followed by another ten-second rest, then four repetitions . . . and so on. To clarify, let's assume you manage seven reps, but cannot make eight . . . then terminate the exercise for that particular workout.

The advantage of this technique is that it pays homage to both the laws of intensity (you do go to failure) and the pump. The accumulated reps bring on a gigantic muscle flush, since you are constantly fighting the time factor, and the total repetitions satisfy the muscle's need for volume.

Cumulative reps were used at the old Santa Monica Muscle Beach in the forties and fifties. Two bodybuilders would face each other on a set of parallel bars. Bodybuilder number one would dip once, then bodybuilder number two would dip once. The first bodybuilder would then dip twice, and the second bodybuilder would dip twice. Turns were taken until one bodybuilder failed to duplicate or beat his rival's repetitions.

In his book, *Special Advice to the Bodybuilder* (Iron Man Publishing Co.), Dennis B. Weis relates a different variation of cumulative repetitions, performed by Chuck Sipes when he was preparing for the Mr. World contest (which he won).

Chuck would perform parallel bar dips, using just body weight, but in a very special way. Dip for one rep, rest two seconds, then do two reps and rest two seconds, then three reps, and rest two seconds . . . and so on. When you can do no more reps, the set is finished. "A goal to aim for," wrote Weis, "is 25 reps on your final set. When you reach this number, you will have done 325 plus reps."

# FORCED REPS

The idea of using forced reps in training has received a lot of publicity over the last few years. The rebirth of the concept was due to Mike Mentzer's push for using high-intensity workouts. It has since been adopted by many champions who have caught the intensity bug. A forced rep simply means continuing to exercise when you can't do another rep on your own. This is accomplished with the help of a workout partner, who places a hand under the bar, or even under your elbows. This used to be called "fingers," and that word would be shouted out by a trainer who sensed impending failure during the last reps of an exercise. The assisting partner must learn to apply evenly balanced help that keeps the weight moving slowly. Too much assistance will negate any effect; too little will cause the bar to stop and ruin the set.

Partner-assisted forced reps can be productive because, like the cheating principle, they can help you over a hard part of an exercise that you could not normally complete. Forced reps are a way of reducing the weight in the middle of an exercise. They are also responsible for increasing overload when you come to a dead end.

Brian Homka assists Scott Wilson with a forced rep as he does an incline bench press.

*Rachel McLish shows good form in a dumbbell curl.*

Rachel McLish, a former Ms. Olympia, once said:

> At best, building quality muscle mass is a difficult proposition for most women bodybuilders. I've been able to develop muscle tissue only by training constantly with the absolute maximum degree of intensity. All my sets are taken to failure and extended past failure by forced and negative reps.

If you have a training partner who understands your needs, you can get just enough boost to slide the bar past the sticking point. This enables you to get extra repetitions and additional intensity, which you would not obtain working on your own.

Partner-assisted reps are not recommended for beginners, or occasional trainers, especially older people. Forced reps are an advanced technique, for those who have an excellent tolerance to physical exercise, who can recuperate adequately, and who are serious about progression. Only a handful of bodybuilders use forced reps all the time. Most use them only as they are completing a training cycle, preparing for a contest, or trying to reach a new plateau.

There are numerous ways to incorporate forced reps into your program. You can just perform them once a week, or every other workout, or you may just want to apply them on bench presses and squats. It's up to you.

# HALF REPS

A repetition of any exercise generally involves a complete movement. For example, a curl is started with the arms in a straight-down vertical position, and the bar is curled until it is under the neck. Half-rep movements involve performing partial reps—an exercise that is restricted to something considerably less than a full-range motion. Partial reps *can* bring something extra to your training.

Bruce Page, who has written more bodybuilding articles than any other man on earth, described training at his local YMCA some 35 years ago:

> I was the weight-training instructor at the time. I always believed in performing an exercise throughout its entire range of movement. Now there was this guy at the YMCA who *always* did half reps in his curls and triceps exercises. At first, I used to privately scoff at his sloppy style, but I never actually corrected him, although I was tempted to many times. Anyway here I was doing full-range arm movements, and not exactly getting earth-shattering results, but this guy was growing like crazy, and he never did a full movement—ever! It wasn't too long before I changed my mind about half reps, and although I still do full-range movements in all exercises, I find there is value in doing short reps, especially when an added spurt of growth is needed.

Half reps are not practical to use in every exercise, but they can be used in most. The important thing is to remember that half reps work your muscles differently than full-range reps. Also, don't fall into the trap of using light weights. If anything, you should be using heavier weights because you are usually working the strongest part of your muscle when performing half reps. If you use light weights, then you are indulging in "muscle spinning." Today we term this practice "pumping up," and it's only done at contest time before going on stage, or prior to a photo session, to give temporary size.

The greatest practitioner of half reps is Sergio Oliva. Almost all his training is done in this way. His curls never start from the straight-arm position, and they stop just after the lower arms pass the parallel-to-floor position. In the bench press and standing press, Sergio never locks his arms. Paradoxically, unlike most bodybuilders who perform half squats (thighs parallel to floor), Sergio has always preferred the full squat. (He's not alone. Tom "Mr. Thighs" Platz also likes full squats.)

Partial reps are not the secret of *every* champion's success, but they do offer a new *feel* to an exercise, and as such can help to stimulate additional growth at a time when your muscles may need a change.

# PEAK CONTRACTION

Since the name of the game is contraction, this principle has got to have an up-front advantage. We know that best progress is made when a maximum number of muscle fibres are contracted. This is done by working a muscle over its full range with particular emphasis in the contracted position.

Peak contraction can be defined as an exercise in which the muscle is under its greatest stress from the resistance at the conclusion of each repetition. The regular barbell curl, in which the barbell passes through the most difficult part of the exercise when the forearms are parallel to the floor, is *not* a peak contraction. There is a definite easing up of resistance as the bar approaches the shoulder area. It is the same with most exercises. As the movement is concluded, there is less resistance for the muscles to fight against.

A peak contraction concludes at a time when you are contracted to the limit, and the particular exercise or the machine being used will not let you work or move beyond this contraction. Pure peak-contraction movements include wide-grip upright rows, wide lat-machine pulldowns, triceps kickbacks, standing leg curls, wide-grip bent-over rows, wide-grip chins, 90-degree preacher bench curls, crunches, gravity-boot sit-ups, thigh exten-

*Sergio Oliva*

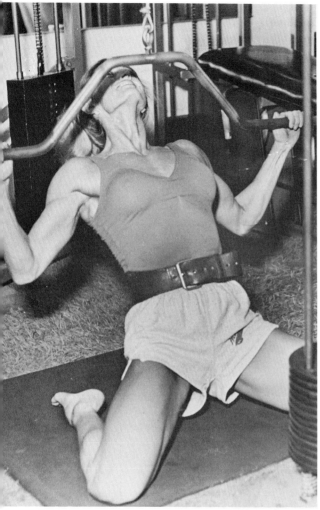
*Dr. Lynne Pirie performs a lat-machine pulldown.*

of nerve impulses are being fired by the muscle.

"My recommendation," said Mike Mentzer, "is that at least one exercise for each muscle group should provide a strong resistance in the contracted position."

Advanced bodybuilders who use peak contractions in some of their exercises agree that the muscles must tense and contract beyond what is imposed by the resistance. In other words, you must consciously squeeze and tense them to their fullest at the conclusion of each peak contraction.

# SLO-MO REPS

Let's accept the fact right now that there are champion bodybuilders who make progress by doing all their reps quickly. And there are those who prefer to feel the exercise more thoroughly by performing the repetitions slowly. Actually, more women than men use slo-mo reps. The reason? Using low-speed repetitions cuts out the creation of any momentum movement, which invariably allows the exerciser to use more weight. Women outnumber their male counterparts in their willingness to sacrifice heavier weights for improved exercise form.

In reality, if a repetition is drawn out enough, both the positive and the negative action, then it gives an effect of almost doubling your reps. Certainly a set will take much longer to complete. Arthur Jones, the inventor of the Nautilus equipment, recommends slow, deliberate repetitions to create maximum usefulness from an exercise.

According to Dr. John Kalas, Chief of Pathology, West Volusia County Hospital, Florida: "The best results are to be had from performing your reps in a *slow and deliberate* fashion." The weight should leave the starting position slowly, with no sudden jerk or thrust, continued in a like manner to the top, where there should be a pause before lowering slowly and under control.

sions, and incline triceps stretches. There are scores of exercises that can be altered to peak contraction simply by altering angles of benches, pulleys, and weights in relation to your body.

For example, Vince Gironda turns a calf raise into a peak-contraction exercise by having his students face the opposite way on a hack machine, holding the slide handles while performing heel raises. By using a lat machine, and lying under it in a supine position (on your back), you can do a useful peak-contraction pulley curl.

Few training methods make more use of the mind than peak-contraction movements. You need pinpoint concentration at the conclusion of each repetition when the maximum number

Since, in this book, I also deal with the usefulness of speed reps, you can readily see the contradiction of advice. The irony is that there is no single way to progress in this sport. Bodybuilding is almost infinitely complex; where argument is produced for one method over another, there is often tangible evidence to show that both can be used successfully if employed with a positive attitude and self-confidence. There's always someone who can break even the most sacred rule and yet proceed to ultimate success.

*Reid Schindle uses a rope for triceps pulldowns.*

# PYRAMID REPS

Virtually every top bodybuilder uses the pyramid system for bench presses and squats, and about 80 percent of others use this system on all moderately heavy movements (incline bench presses, lat pulldowns, shoulder presses, thigh extensions, calf raises, etc.).

You start the pyramid system by beginning with a light set using high repetitions (12–15) to warm up the muscles. As each set is performed, more weight is added and less repetitions are used. This is done with each set until only a few reps are possible. You then start to decrease the weight again and perform higher repetitions as the exercise is ended.

The pyramid method is very workable and invariably gives good results. The reason for this may be due to the fact that high and low reps are involved. The blood is put into the muscle area with the initial sets because of the higher reps; the muscle fibres are then hit hard by the low-rep heavy sets and the body part is forced to a maximum pump with a set or two of higher reps. A typical pyramid schedule for the bench press might look like the following:

| Set | Reps | Pounds |
|-----|------|--------|
| 1 | 20 | 120 |
| 2 | 20 | 150 |
| 3 | 8 | 170 |
| 4 | 6 | 190 |
| 5 | 6 | 210 |
| 6 | 3 | 230 |
| 7 | 8 | 150 |
| 8 | 15 | 120 |

A pyramid routine for the squat exercise could be set out as in the following progression:

| Set | Reps | Pounds |
|-----|------|--------|
| 1 | 20 | 145 |
| 2 | 12 | 185 |
| 3 | 10 | 225 |
| 4 | 8 | 265 |
| 5 | 8 | 265 |
| 6 | 6 | 285 |
| 7 | 12 | 215 |
| 8 | 15 | 205 |

Occasionally, a person using the pyramid system will work up to a limit-single attempt, but this should be done infrequently. Be careful not to cause an injury when doing a limit rep.

# REP PAUSING

This method should not be confused with *rest-pause* training, which is dealt with on page 78. Rep pausing is when you stop in the middle of a set (or at any other time during the set, for that matter) to recoup more energy to continue. Actually, this pause can be for any of the following reasons:

1. To pay back an oxygen debt. People who perform high reps of squats often pause as they near the end of a set, to recover from insufficient oxygen. Once they have gulped air for 15–20 seconds they can continue to the end of a set.
2. To allow lactic acid buildup to subside. Sometimes the pain can be unbearable, and a suitably brief pause will allow some relief—enough to continue for several more important reps. Larry Scott would often do this when training his calves. He would bend his knees and stop exercising for 15 seconds. Then he would continue until the end of the set.
3. To reassert yourself mentally. Samir Bannout and Sergio Oliva, both Mr. Olympias in their bodybuilding careers, practice this method. If Sergio finds himself getting a little bored in the middle of a set or exercise, he stops, concentrates, and reasserts his mental commitment to complete his reps. Samir Bannout pauses when performing thigh extensions, an exercise which he tends to do in high repetitions. He stops just as he reaches the edge of the pain threshold; he reasserts himself during the pause, and then barrels through the pain barrier to complete the set.

*Samir Bannout and Mohamed Makkawy*

*Chris Dickerson demonstrates a leg press.*

# NEGATIVE REPS

A negative repetition is that part of an exercise when the weight is lowered to the starting position of the movement. When you resist gravity but allow it to slowly win, you are performing a negative action. Every bodybuilder uses negative reps to a certain extent, but what is really meant by the term is the definite control of a weight as it descends after each repetition.

Mike Mentzer takes the performance of negative reps even further. He exercises until failure (until he cannot perform another repetition) and then continues to benefit by employing the negative aspect of training. This is done by using one of the following methods:

1. To have a training partner help raise the weight so that you can repeatedly resist on its downward (negative) movement.
2. To cheat the weight up by using body mo-

tion and momentum, and consequently maneuver the weight into a position suitable for performing negative repetitions.
3. To use an apparatus in such a way that your arms and legs can combine to raise a weight against gravity, yet only one limb is used in lowering the same weight. (Leg press: raise weight with two legs, lower with one. Calf raise: heel raises with two legs, lower with one. Single-arm dumbbell curl: use your free hand to provide the curling arm with assistance, lower without aid. Leg extension: raise weight with two legs, lower with one. Chins: use both arms to lift the body, lower with one.)

It is generally conceded that negative reps are very depleting. Some champions do not use them at all, whereas a few use them all the time. The vast majority, however, employ them in their schedules once a week, and then only on a few key exercises, such as chest and shoulder movements in the sitting, incline, or lying position. For those utilizing high-intensity methods, forced reps may be the answer. Use them moderately, depending on your tolerance to intense training.

*Proof that isotension works is evidenced in the muscle definition of Tom Platz's right thigh.*

# ISOTENSION

Writer Bill Reynolds has been quoted as saying that isotension is one of the secrets of bodybuilders that puts the finishing touches to their physiques. What is isotension? It is the tensing of a muscle either during or at the completion of a repetition. In fact, isotension, the deliberate flexing of a muscle area, can be performed between sets or even in front of a mirror. Eugene Sandow used this technique over 60 years ago to tone his muscles when he couldn't get to the weights. Charles Atlas recommended it in his mail-order tensile-contraction courses, which sold millions of copies worldwide.

To perform isotension movements, flex a chosen muscle as hard as you can during the last three or four repetitions of an exercise. Forget about lifting the weight. The idea is to get the muscles to become excessively stressed.

When you use isotension apart from your workout—at home, for example—then hold each flex for about six seconds, rest a few moments, and then repeat the procedure. You will etch in some real striations if you make a habit of isotension.

Don't confuse isotension with low-intensity muscle flexing or muscle control in which muscles are wiggled, rolled, or isolated in split-second contractions. Isotension is the complete flexing (even to the point of cramping), then loosening and relaxing of the muscle. As Joe Weider once said (he probably coined the term "isotension"):

> The isotension action is explosive. Stimuli are fired into the muscle when it's at peak contraction. The muscle tissue reacts by practically climbing out of the skin. It is a marvelous muscle-refining technique.

With practice, you can apply this principle to every muscle, tensing the thighs, biceps, triceps, and pecs in a variety of positions. Actually, the act of posing is a form of isotension. Tom Platz practiced it more on his right thigh

*Curls on a preacher bench . . . Bill Richardson-style*

than his left (giving posing exhibitions all over the world), and the extra tension has grooved in phenomenal thigh detail that brings astonished gasps from audiences. He can't duplicate this effect with his left thigh. Yes, isotension works!

# CONTINUOUS TENSION

Continuous tension can be described as a practice whereby you maintain a tough work load as you lift a weight or exercise on a machine through its range of motion. You can maintain tension by slowing up the momentum when the going gets easy. Continuous tension, of course, can also be brought into play by applying the aforementioned principle of isotension.

Those training in the final stages of precontest preparation may find particular value in combining continuous tension with peak contraction. In this way, ultimate detail and separation will appear in your muscles as the contest date approaches, always assuming that superfluous fat is removed from under the skin by a strict calorie-controlled diet.

The most common method of applying continuous tension to your training is to avoid locking any joints during your exercises. Locked elbows or knee joints usually, though not always, constitute relief from muscle tension. Avoid doing this in squats, presses, chins, curls, supine presses, triceps extensions, thigh curls, dips, incline presses—and you will bring continuous tension into play. It's a worthwhile technique.

*Franco Columbu*

# BURNS

The term "burns" in relation to bodybuilding was first uttered in a small hardcore bodybuilding gym in North Hollywood. More precisely, it came from the lips of the Iron Guru, Vince Gironda. His star pupil, Larry Scott, used them to add to the maximum overload he placed on his muscles each and every set.

"I am often asked what 'burns' are!" said Gironda. "They are the addition of three or four half or quarter reps at the end of a set of exercise. The motion involved is usually only 2–3 inches (5–8 cm). The idea is to maximize the pump before ending a set."

In fact, burns are not used in every exercise. They are, however, used extensively in Scott curls, calf raises, triceps pressdowns, flye motions, lat pulls, crunches, and dips. Burns enable the trainer to continue an exercise when another rep cannot be performed. They keep the blood in the area a few seconds longer. More fibres are recruited and fired off. More growth is stimulated.

Tom Platz, writing in his book *Pro-Style Bodybuilding* (Sterling Publishing, Co., Inc., NY) made this announcement:

> I probably think more about "burns" and tension in my muscles than about anything else when I work out. I use burns to build up the pain and then put it out of my mind and build it up even higher. When I can't do any more full reps, I'll do half or partial reps, which defines burns for me.

*Bertil Fox and Sergio Oliva*

*Carla Temple*

# "21" SYSTEM

This is a method which was popular on the West Coast bodybuilding scene in the fifties and sixties. Let's use the barbell curl again as an example.

Begin by selecting a weighted barbell that you can curl eight or ten times. Proceed to curl it to the halfway position only—seven reps. After this, without any pause whatsoever, do seven more curls from the halfway position to the top where the bar reaches the base of the neck. Finally, again without pause, perform seven *complete* curls using the fullest range of movement possible. That's the 21 movement.

This technique should not be performed for every exercise, but certainly it can be used for most. It is especially effective in arm, back, shoulder, and chest exercises. Writer Bruce Page claimed to have put a full inch on his biceps, when all else failed, by using the 21 barbell-curl system for five weeks. You may obtain such remarkable results, but then again, it could be the challenge your biceps need to stimulate them into new growth. You'll never know if you don't give it a shot!

# TEMPO CHANGING

Reps are usually performed at a fairly even pace. Some bodybuilders even go so far as to say that they should be done with an even rhythm and cadence. But as you are by now becoming aware, rules are made to be broken. There is shock value in changing pace in midstream. Certainly the muscles get a different effect when they are worked at a variety of rep tempos.

Oddly enough, this is never written about in magazine articles, yet many bodybuilders have developed habits of changing their pace halfway through their sets. Sometimes they'll work faster. At other times, a deliberate effort is made to slow everything up. It is just another way of alleviating boredom, keeping the muscles off balance, to cause them to overcompensate for the "shock," and grow even bigger.

*Carla Dunlap and Tony Pearson*

# Part IV
# PERFORMING THE PERFECT SET

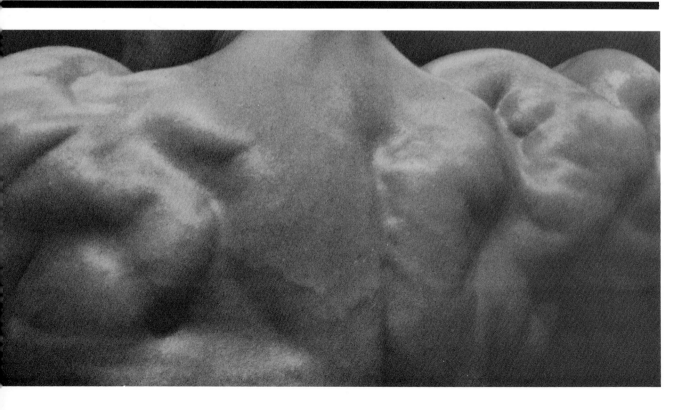

*Ali Mala*

Your workout routine is made up of a combination of sets, which, in turn, are comprised of a specific number of reps. The effectiveness of your routine is largely determined, not by the quantity of sets and reps you do, but by the quality level of your set performance.

Robby Robinson, nicknamed the Black Prince of Bodybuilding, said the following about set performance:

> The perfect set would mean more to me if it came when I was hitting a muscle from an entirely new angle. This perfect set would flow from a combination of perfect concentration, perfect tension, perfect tempo, and a perfect range of motion. It's an extremely difficult set to do, but it gets results!

Let's take a look at the many ways of performing a set.

# STRAIGHT SETS

This system is the most common and one of the most effective methods of training for beginners, intermediates, and advanced bodybuilders. A straight set is a series of repetitions performed continuously until the last rep is completed. Each successive rep involves more and more muscle fibres until the set is finished.

The practice of straight sets has been prevalent for a long time now. The following account was made by bodybuilding writer Harry B. Paschall:

> About 1940 a number of lavishly muscled supermen appeared on the American scene,

following the inception of the annual Mr. America award, which began in 1939. We spent a good bit of time backstage at these shows, watching the bodybuilders warm up for the contest, and found they had hit upon a new technique for inflating the tissues with blood. They did innumerable sets of curls, bench presses, and dumbbell movements, and they had grown some impressive lumps. The cult grew rapidly, and its center was on the Pacific Coast (Santa Monica). Today the idea of using a group of series exercises (sets) is standard in every gym catering to musclebuilders.

*Robby Robinson, nicknamed the "Black Prince."*

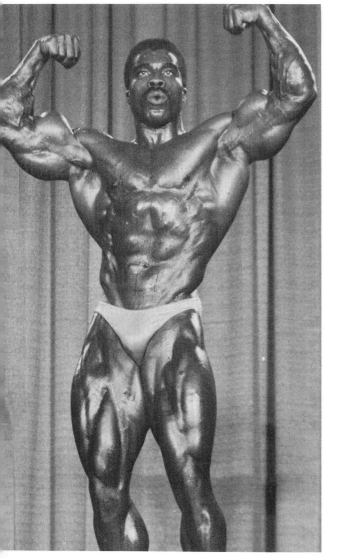

Don Ross

# DIMINISHING SETS

The system of diminishing sets can be applied to any series of exercises. The idea behind this method is to perform 100 reps in as few sets as possible, with rest time between sets at a minimum. You will probably need to do several sets to do 100 reps at first—as many as ten. Try to cut down to four sets, at which time you should increase your poundage.

You don't have to do 25 reps per set—the first set may be 40 reps, 25 for the second, 20 for the third, and 15 for the last. Squeeze out as many reps as possible in each set. Don't baby yourself in the early sets to save energy for later.

Bodybuilding requires variety to shock muscles into growth as they adapt to stress. Diminishing sets will give your muscles a whole new type of training intensity. In order to meet the challenge, your muscles will get bigger!

According to Mr. Universe Don Ross: "It is best to plan a routine consisting of one or two exercises per body part." The following program is ideal to use with diminishing sets:

| Monday, Wednesday, Friday | Tuesday, Thursday, Saturday |
|---|---|
| Bench Press | Hyperextension |
| Incline Flye | Leg Extension |
| Upright Row | Leg Curl |
| Wide-grip Pulldown | Crunch |
| Bent-over Dumbbell Row | Heel Raise |
| Barbell Curl | |
| Triceps Pushdown | |
| Wrist Curl | |

# MUSCLE PRIORITY

Few people would deny that they have more energy at the beginning of a workout than at the end. True enough, some bodybuilders pace themselves sufficiently during their training so they can give each body part a good workout. However, they are strongest at the start.

The muscle-priority method is a system by which you train your most underdeveloped

*Backstage preparation before a contest (left to right): Greg DeFerro, Johnny Fuller, Bill Grant, Tim Belknap, and John Terilli.*

body part *first* in the routine, at a time when your energy and enthusiasm levels are at a peak.

When reminded to train a poorly responding body part *first* in the routine, an experienced bodybuilder might say that it doesn't fit in with his usual training order. For example, if his arms are in need of more size, then it may not seem *right* to train them first in the workout for the simple reason that he may not be able to do justice to the other body parts after overtiring the arms. This is a very real possibility since the arms are used extensively in shoulder, chest, and back work.

If a bodybuilder's arms are *really* in need of development, then I recommend the muscle-priority system, including a few exercises which do *not* work the arms (such as thigh, abdominal, and calf work) between the arm movements. This will serve to rest the arm area, and will also allow some recuperation time, making it possible to do justice to other body parts.

*Tony Pearson*

Obviously, although there is a case for *not* using the muscle-priority system for arm training, it fits in very well with just about every other muscle group. Even to this day, Bill Pearl trains his abdominals first in his routine. Mohamed Makkawy usually devotes the first 40 minutes of his workout to his back, and Tony Pearson hammers his calves first, while he is fresh and ready to go. Both Arnold Schwarzenegger and Lou Ferrigno made amazing gains in their lower legs by training them first in each workout.

# COMPOUND SETS

Also known as giant sets, this method is definitely an advanced way of training the muscles that can either bolster your gains sharply or throw you into the overtraining syndrome.

A compound set is the consecutive performance of four (or even five) exercises for one body part, followed by a brief rest period. For example, an entire chest routine might be the following (which should be performed three times):

| Compound Set | Reps |
|---|---|
| Bench Press | 10 |
| Incline Bench Press | 10 |
| Flat Bench Flye | 10 |
| Cable Crossover | 10 |
| Rest (two minutes) | |

The following is a compound set for the shoulders (performed three times):

| Compound Set | Reps |
|---|---|
| Press behind Neck | 10 |
| Alternate Dumbbell Press | 10 |
| Upright Row | 10 |
| Lateral Raise | 10 |
| Rest (two minutes) | |

Rick Wayne was one of the first bodybuilders to successfully incorporate compound sets into his training. He would enter the gym and set up all the weights that he intended to use in advance so that there would be a minimum distance between the different workout positions. Then he would take a couple of minutes to go through the compound set in his mind before attacking the exercises.

# DESCENDING SETS

Known in Britain as the triple-drop method, this practice is theoretically one of the most demanding of all. A descending set, as the name suggests, entails the reduction of weight during the performance of a specific exercise, when a set becomes impossible to complete.

Let's look at the bench press to illustrate the method. Begin with a barbell loaded with sufficient weight to allow four or five good reps. When you cannot perform any more, have two workout partners simultaneously remove about 20 percent of the weight (one disc from each side). Continue doing reps until once more you reach a point of failure. Then again have your partners remove 20 percent more weight. Complete the set by continuing until you cannot lift this final load.

It is important that the weights are removed smoothly, with utmost speed, and in unison to not upset your balance. Don't stop to rest after your training partners have taken off the weights. With a little ingenuity, this principle can be used in just about every exercise. If you are using a machine that has a pin for selecting various weights, then the reducing job is made even simpler. Only one training partner is required to pull out the pin and insert it at a lesser weight.

When you use this demanding method be aware that you can be almost tripling your usual intensity level. Accordingly, you should perform less overall sets to achieve worthwhile results.

*Casey Viator does some heavy work on a calf machine.*

*Lori Bowen-Rice*

# UP-AND-DOWN-THE-RACK SETS

Vince Gironda, coauthor of the book *Unleashing the Wild Physique*, popularized this technique, calling it one of the most effective ways of building up the biceps. The method is not practical for the bodybuilder who trains at home, unless he has a dumbbell rack with a complete assortment of weights.

Here's how the method works: Stand near a dumbbell rack and curl the 20-pound dumbbells (or another low weight to begin with) five reps. Move up to the 25-pounders for five reps and then to the 30-pounders, the 35-pounders, and so on, up the rack. Advanced men will go up to 70- or 80-pound dumbbells; women may only be able to use 40-pound dumbbells. The point is to go as heavy as you can while still performing four or five repetitions. After you reach your limit, decrease the poundage, still using the same number of repetitions, making sure that you take no more than a five- or ten-second rest between each set. Obviously, you need a set-up rack to follow this method. It would be pointless to use one pair of dumbbells for this training procedure because far too much time would be taken to change the weights.

# TRISETS

With trisets, you do one set each of three exercises, one right after the other, with very little rest between sets—no more, in fact, than it takes to change exercises. At the completion of the three exercises, rest for 60 seconds, then do a second cycle. Repeat this a third time for three trisets. Very advanced trainers may graduate to four complete trisets.

Trisets can be used in two distinct ways. You may use the multi-angular approach to hit different sections of a muscle group, or you may attack a muscle from a uni-angular position.

An example of hitting a muscle group from different angles would be to do a deltoid (shoulder) triset involving one exercise for each of the three deltoid heads. For instance, the rear deltoid could be worked with bent-over flyes, the side deltoid with lateral raises, and the front deltoid with alternate dumbbell raises. Likewise, you could hit different parts of the biceps by changing the angle on a preacher bench from 90 degrees (upright) to 45 degrees to 25 degrees.

The uni-angular triset is even more concentrated. You are hitting the same area of a muscle to encourage growth in that area alone. For instance, you could concentrate on building the biceps peak if you triset 90-degree preacher curls with bent-over barbell concentration curls and single-arm seated concentration curls. Alternatively, you could really single out the lower thigh area with a triset of sissy squats, hack lifts, and front squats.

Ideally, a triset should be set up before you start. This is not always practical in crowded gyms. If you have to wait for someone to finish a set before you can complete your triset, the effectiveness will be lost.

# SUPERSETS

According to bodybuilder Boyer Coe: "Supersets are for bodybuilders who have been training long enough to require added work to increase their strength and muscularity."

A superset is the alternation of two exercises—with a minimum amount of rest—that work opposing muscle groups. A typical superset would be the alternation of barbell curls (for the biceps) with lying extensions (for the triceps). The performance of two exercises for one body part, such as the biceps, is also a superset. You could alternate seated in-

*Mr. Universe Boyer Coe is an advocate of supersets.*

cline dumbbell curls (which stress the long head of the biceps) with concentration curls (which apply relatively equal stress to the overall biceps).

Supersets are invariably what a bodybuilder turns to when more intensity is required. Superset training adds a new dimension to muscle growth. It gives a development that is dissimilar to the growth obtained from conventional (slower) training. Supersets build not only the muscle fibres, but also the cell's internal components, which make increased muscle mass possible. Additionally, because supersets are performed in rapid succession, they improve your cardiovascular efficiency, metabolic rate, and increase the fat-burning process.

Supersets also reduce the amount of workout time needed to completely fatigue a muscle. However, this time-efficient method is not for beginners, who could be vulnerable to injury by supersetting, since muscle tissues and tendons are not accustomed to the more in-tense overload effects provided by this technique.

Experimentation with supersets can unfold a variety of possibilities. You can reverse the order of the exercises, do different combinations, or use heavy and light supersets with high reps or low reps. You can even employ different superset combinations for the same body part on two consecutive training days.

# REST-PAUSE SETS

The renewed popularity of the rest-pause system was brought about by one man: Mike Mentzer. "Rest-pause training is the most advanced, intensive, stressful form of training to date. Its effects are immediate and very dramatic," he said. Actually, Mentzer cautions

*Gladys Portugues observes Val Phillips as she does an incline dumbbell press.*

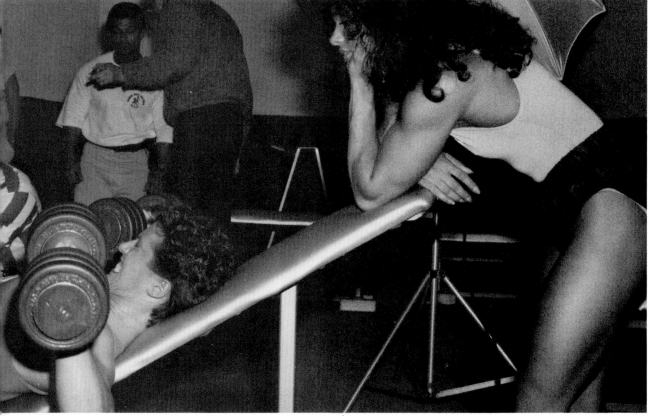

against overtraining when using the rest-pause method. Beginners and intermediates would be well advised not to use the principle until they get into more advanced training.

Let's use the Universal bench press apparatus to illustrate rest-pause training. Select a weight in which you can perform only one repetition. After you have completed the single rep, rest for 10–15 seconds (to recover strength). Complete another repetition with the same weight followed by another rest of 10–15 seconds. Do this for five to eight reps. You may require that your training partner decrease the weight resistance slightly after three or four reps, which is normal.

Rest-pause training works best with large muscle groups, especially those exercises involving multi-joint action. It can, however, be used with any exercise. If free weights are used, they have to be returned to the rack (in the case of squats, bench presses, dumbbell presses, dumbbell curls, etc.) between repetitions. In the case of barbell exercises, you could return the bar to a bench to avoid having to pick it up from the floor between rest-pause repetitions.

# STAGGERED SETS

The main advantage of this technique is the elimination of wasted time. You get more done in a given time frame.

As a bodybuilder, you will add mass more quickly if you devote most of your energy towards training the largest muscle areas of the body—the back, thighs, chest, etc. Often, however, after doing justice to such areas, you have little energy (and inclination) at the end of the workout for abs, calves, forearms, or neck work. Unless these areas are worked regularly they will definitely begin to lag behind.

With staggered sets, the small muscle groups can be worked hard without robbing your body of energy. This can be achieved by

John Terilli

staggering a set for a major muscle with a set for a minor one. For example, after a heavy set of bench presses, perform a set of forearm curls for the lower arms. The action will not interfere with your bench workout; it will act as a rest period for the pectorals. The smaller muscle group requires much less energy.

Staggered sets are not used so extensively today as they were in the forties and fifties, but many trainers still use the system . . . and not always just to save time. Because you are taking advantage of fresh energy levels, you are able to put more into the minor exercises that would normally be relegated to the low-energy end of the workout.

*Andreas Cahling*

Reportedly, Frank Zane, during his Olympia training, would often stagger thigh-extension movements with various other body parts. He felt that he needed the specialization to improve the definition and separation in his thighs. Rather than waste time resting, Frank would perform up to 20 sets of thigh extensions between heavier sets of back and chest work.

Many bodybuilders, including Reg Park, Arnold Schwarzenegger, Tony Pearson, and Robby Robinson, have used staggered sets of calf work to augment their lower leg development. For example, heavy calf-machine training may be used two or three days a week, plus two sessions of staggered (lighter) calf raises on off days. The extra stimulation of staggered sets can make all the difference.

# PRE-EXHAUST TECHNIQUE

Many people are aware of the fact that I invented the pre-exhaust technique. I worked out the theory in my mind long before putting it into practice. It is a method that is widely used today and is credited with breaking the sticking points of numerous bodybuilders.

The original theory was materialized out of necessity, for I desperately wanted to widen my shoulders, although I had performed thousands of sets of presses in all the barbell and dumbbell variations, and duly followed these heavy sets with a variety of dumbbell laterals, workout after workout. I just could not work my shoulders hard enough to make them sore the next day, which would indicate muscle growth. I clearly defined the problem as needing to work the deltoid cap more vigorously than it had ever been done before. How could I get to the deepest fibres? How could I totally exhaust my deltoids so they would grow?

When I was 20 years old I had thought of the solution: Work the shoulders first by tiring

*Corinna Everson, Rachel McLish, and Inger Zetterqvist line up at a recent Ms. Olympia contest.*

them out with an isolation movement and then go to the limit with a general (combination) exercise such as the press behind neck. In order to keep up with the fresh triceps muscles, the already tired deltoid cap would have to really dig down deep to get the power to hoist the resistance. Deeper muscle fibres would be brought into play.

That night I tried out my theory and I could actually feel the deltoids suffering from the unusual practice of following a lighter shoulder isolation exercise with a combination movement. The next day my shoulders were sore to the bone. I was ecstatic!

I wrote to Joseph Weider, a well-known name in the bodybuilding field. To my surprise,

Joe wrote back, asking me to elaborate on my discovery, which he would consider purchasing and incorporating into the Weider system, if it were suitable.

Six years later, after Weider failed to take a position on my pre-exhaust system, I wrote a short article for *Iron Man* magazine. The publisher held the manuscript for almost two years, but eventually it appeared in 1968 (vol. 27 issue 4).

Pre-exhaustion had arrived! No one seemed to get too excited, but pretty soon Arthur Jones, originator of the famous Nautilus machines, was promoting the principle.

Others to use the pre-exhaustion technique successfully were Mr. America Steve Michalik,

*Frank Richards of England*

and more recently, Mike Mentzer and his brother Ray. Both men have made quite remarkable progress with the principle. Boyer Coe, Scott Wilson, Rachel McLish, and dozens of other champions use the method regularly.

So what is the pre-exhaust system? It is the battering of a specific muscle with a carefully chosen isolation exercise immediately followed by a combination movement. Let's use the pecs as an example. As you may know, the triceps are the weak links involved in many chest exercises. In other words, when you do dips, bench presses, or incline presses, the triceps are worked hard and the pectorals only moderately. This means that your triceps will grow more rapidly than your chest. That's fine

if you already have a big chest, but if you want to develop those pecs, then nothing will do it quite as fast as the pre-exhaust method.

The way to get around the "weak-link" triceps is to isolate the pecs first with an exercise like cable crossovers or dumbbell flyes, where the triceps are not directly involved. After a hard set, performing the exercises to the point of failure, proceed *immediately* to the second combination exercise, such as incline presses or bench presses. At the time of doing the presses, the triceps will be *temporarily* stronger than the pectorals, which will be in a state of near exhaustion from the first isolation exercise.

The following exercises can be used for pre-exhaust training:

**Thighs**
*Isolation Movements*
Leg Extension, Roman Chair Squats
*Combination Movements*
Squat, Front Squat, Hack Slide

**Chest**
*Isolation Movements*
Flat Flye, Pulley Crossover, Pec-Deck Flye
*Combination Movements*
Supine Bench Press, Dumbbell Bench Press

**Upper Chest**
*Isolation Movement*
Incline Flye
*Combination Movements*
Incline Bench Press, Incline Dumbbell Press

**Lower Chest**
*Isolation Movements*
Decline Flye, Decline Cable Crossover
*Combination Movements*
Wide-grip Parallel Bar Dip, Decline Bench Press, Decline Dumbbell Bench Press

**Thigh Biceps**
*Isolation Movements*
Lying Leg Curl (machine), Standing Leg Curl
*Combination Movement*
Upside-down Squat (with gravity boots)

**Waist**
*Isolation Movement*
Crunch
*Combination Movements*
Hanging Leg Raise, Inverted Sit-up (with gravity boots)

## Back
*Isolation Movements*
Nautilus Pullover, Barbell Pullover, Parallel Bar Shrugs
*Combination Movements*
Bent-over Row, Chin to Chest, T-bar Row

## Trapezius
*Isolation Movements*
Shrugs (dumbbells, barbell, calf machine, or bench)
*Combination Movements*
Upright Row, Smith-machine Clean

## Biceps
*Isolation Movement*
Preacher Bench Curl (dumbbell or barbell)
*Combination Movement*
Close-undergrip Chin

## Triceps
*Isolation Movements*
Pulley Pressdown, Standing Barbell Extension
*Combination Movements*
Narrow-grip Bench Press, Parallel Bar Dip

## Forearms
*Isolation Movements*
Reverse Wrist Curl
*Combination Movement*
Reverse Curl

## Calves
*Isolation Movements*
Toe Raise (leg-press machine), Standing Calf Raise, Donkey Calf Raise
*Combination Movements*
Rope Jumping, High Rebounder Jump

## Rear Shoulders
*Isolation Movements*
Bent-over Flye, Bent-over Cable Flye, Pec-Deck (reverse position)
*Combination Movements*
Bent-over Barbell Row, Seated Cable Row

## Side Shoulders
*Isolation Movements*
Lateral Raise, Cable Side Raise
*Combination Movements*
Upright Row (wide grip), Press behind Neck

*Pirjo Haapalo performs Pec-Deck flyes for her chest muscles.*

# TRAINING FREQUENCY

Training frequency is important. It has to fit in with your job, energy level, family life, recuperative ability, overall condition, and, of course, it has to be in line with the goals you have set yourself.

Up until 1960 there was only one training frequency. You trained *three times a week*—Mondays, Wednesdays, and Fridays—period. Actually, this is a slight exaggeration, but the training options that we know about today didn't exist back then. Today almost everyone has a different theory on how many times to train each week.

Jon Aranita

Bodybuilders often base their workouts around the seven-day week because their work, school, and daily lives, etc., are also based around this same cycle. Some gyms are not even open on Saturdays or Sundays, while others set aside only certain nights for men's training, leaving alternative evenings for women's workouts. If you train at home, or if you are a member of a gym that is open seven days a week, then you can arrange your workout frequency as you wish.

In order to develop properly, muscles must be trained at least twice weekly, up to and including three times weekly. The more frequently you train muscles using the overload system, the faster they will grow *providing* you recuperate completely between workouts. This proviso is not to be taken lightly. The vast majority of men and women trainers do not make their best gains training each body part *too* frequently.

Steve Davis and Heidi Miller

Remember that progressive-resistance bodybuilding with weights is the most demanding system in existence of overloading the muscles. Your body requires time for recuperation, usually 48–72 hours. This does not mean that your workouts must be spaced 48–72 hours apart. However, you shouldn't work the same body part within that critical period. This means splitting your routine into two or three parts, performing one part one day and other parts at a later time, and so on. When you split a routine you can work out two successive days (or more) in a row because you don't exercise the same muscles each day. One day you may work your back and arms, the next day you train your chest and legs.

Now let's look at the different methods of training frequency.

## Every-Other-Day Split

Tens of thousands of trainers have found this method very satisfactory. It is a super way to build size and power during the off-season period.

This system is one in which you perform half your workout one day, followed by a complete rest the next day. The following day you train the other half of your body and rest again the next day. As you can see, this system does not fit into the conventional seven-day cycle. It is strictly for home trainers or for those who are members of commercial gymnasiums that are open every day of the week.

The great advantage of the every-other-day split method is that once it is underway you never have problems with recuperation. It invariably works out that you are fully recovered and raring to go when your next workout is due. A word of warning: Your rest between workouts is *one* day. Do not ever rest for two days straight. If this happens, you should make up the missed workout by training two days in a row. It is not a good idea to make this a habit.

## Monday-Wednesday-Friday Routine

Still the most popular of all, this method offers the triple advantage of training the body three times a week, allowing for at least a full

Erika Mes

day's rest between workouts, with the weekends free. This all makes for a very attractive arrangement. You train the entire body each workout. This works well for the beginner who neither does a large number of sets nor a great variety of exercises.

As the beginner becomes an intermediate or advanced bodybuilder, where more sets and exercises are utilized, problems arise. The difficulty is that training the entire body in one workout (shoulders, back, chest, arms, calves, thighs, abdominals, etc.) becomes a chore that cannot always be completed without running out of energy. As a seasoned bodybuilder, you have to do justice to *each* body part. You shouldn't quit training an area until you have exercised it thoroughly, fatiguing it completely.

## Four- and Six-Day Splits

These are very definitely off-season schedules. In other words, they are building-up methods rather than ones that prepare you for the final stages of contest conditioning.

In the four-day split, you work within the confines of the seven-day week. You split your workout into two parts. The simplest way to divide your program is to save all upper-body

*Kay Baxter*

exercises for one training session and all lower-body (leg) movements for another. Alternatively, some bodybuilders prefer to do all *pulling* movements (rowing, curling, chins, wrist curls, etc.) one day and all *pushing* movements (presses, triceps, stretches, squats) another day. In truth, all muscles pull, not push, but it seems like they push when you lift away from the body.

Having divided the workout into two equal parts, you perform the first part on Monday, the second part on Tuesday. Wednesday is a rest day. You perform the initial half of the routine on Thursday and on Friday you do the second half again. The weekends are left free. Your complete body is exercised twice weekly, which is enough for most people to develop.

The six-day split leaves you only one day's rest a week. It is more rigorous than the four-day split since instead of working the whole body twice every seven days, you work it three times a week. However, as I suggested earlier, to train the body six days a week all year round is often too much work and can cause an overtrained condition or burnout. Your gains could slow down or even stop altogether.

## Calta Routine

Frank Calta, the Florida-based competitive bodybuilder, formulated his own routine, which he calls "rotation for recuperation." According to this principle, you train just three days a week (usually Mondays, Wednesdays, and Fridays). Again, you divide the workout into two equal parts. You train the first part on Monday, rest Tuesday, train the second part on Wednesday, rest Thursday, train the first half again on Friday, and rest on Saturday and Sunday. Each body part gets trained only one and a half times a week.

"Quite frankly," said Calta, "the amount of people overtraining is pathetic. I have been in the business twelve years and I am now positive that most serious bodybuilders train too frequently and for too long."

Because Calta's method only hits each muscle area twice every eight days, he recommends training with high intensity, using four different exercises per muscle group. In this way the muscles are hit from every angle.

*Deanna Panting of Canada*

## Two-Days-On/One-Day-Off Routine

Split your routine into two fairly equal halves. Perform the first half one day and then the very next day do the second half. The third day is a rest day. The day after resting, begin again with the first half of your routine, following this with the second part. The next day is a rest day again.

This frequency does not give you the weekends free; if that's not a problem, it can be a very workable system.

Since you work out for two successive days with this schedule, it is not advisable to train the same body parts two days in a row. In other words, split your routine so that *different* body parts are worked on successive days. There will be some slight overlapping of exercised muscles since all the muscles are involved to some extent whenever you train.

A suggested routine is to work back, legs, and biceps one day, and shoulders, abs, chest, and triceps on other days (the pull/push split). However, even though there is some obvious overlapping involved, the following type of split is very effective: chest, back, and arms one day; shoulders, legs, and abs the next.

## Three-Day Split

A routine doesn't have to be divided into just two parts. There can be value in dividing it into *three*. For example, you could train shoulders and chest one day, legs and back the next day, and biceps, triceps, and waist the third. It would take six consecutive workouts, resting on the seventh day, to accomplish two workouts a week for each body part. The advantage, of course, is that when you only train one or two body parts per workout you can hammer those parts both hard and long. More sets and exercises for those muscle areas can be performed. If you can take it, the three-way split, six-day workout, is ideal for advanced men and women who want to hit their muscles hard with at least three, four, or even five exercises for each part. But it's hard work. Kal Szkalak and Carolyn Cheshire have both used this method extensively.

*Kal Szkalak*

# Back-Cycling Routine

According to physique star Don Ross, "Back cycling is one of the most important principles through which you can achieve continuous gains."

As your training progresses, there is a tendency for your workouts to get longer. You feel a need to add exercises, and a desire to add sets. To complicate matters, a bodybuilder hates to drop an exercise from a routine. It may mean a loss of muscle size. Soon the workout is over three hours long. "What do you do then?" asks Don Ross. "Train for *four* hours a day?"

He found a solution. After training each body part for 20–24 sets each, he cuts back to just three sets of each exercise. This brings his routine down to around nine sets per body part, but it results in heavier weights used in all exercises and improved muscular development.

The beauty of weight training is that you can maintain a strength plateau with a minimum number of sets. It may take years to achieve a 400-pound bench press, and the ultimate performance of thousands of sets, yet once achieved, you can hold that magic figure with a minimum amount of sets.

Don't forget that increased strength is indicative of increased muscular development. True, some persons with smaller muscles are stronger than others with bigger muscles, but this is due to advantageous leverage factors. When your strength develops, muscle size will occur simultaneously, or shortly thereafter.

In essence, back cycling reduces the length of your workout while it maintains what you've gained. It could be seen as a method of taking one step back and two forward.

*An incline dumbbell press as demonstrated by Gladys Portugues*

# Part V

# THE
# WORKOUT
# ROUTINES

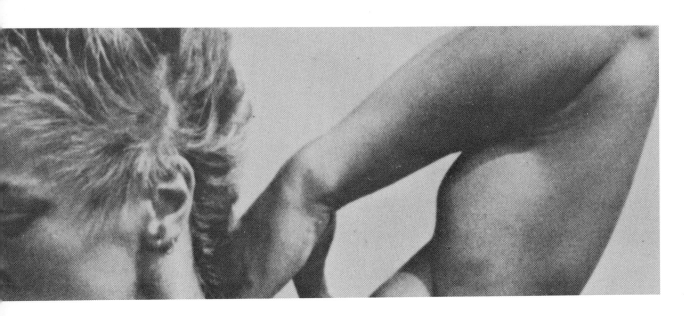

*Asa Gillberg*

**Y**our routine is the heart of the matter in bodybuilding. It's your program for results! There are literally hundreds of thousands of routines, and the potential exists for millions of variations. Your job as a bodybuilder or fitness enthusiast is to decide what your immediate goals are. Once that is done, a routine can be chosen to meet your aims. The following routines represent the widest variety to help you achieve exactly what you want from progressive-resistance exercise. Whether you are male or female, short or tall, fat or thin, beginner or advanced, young or not so young . . . there is a routine here for you.

# BEGINNER'S ROUTINE

Those new to bodybuilding should be aware that a body needs to be *slowly* introduced to weight training. You cannot suddenly throw yourself into an intensive routine, forcing out the repetitions . . . to do so would cause an injury, and at the very least you will bring about painful muscle soreness that will prevent you from proper training. It is important to use good exercise style, and use a weight that is well within your ability to lift without undue strain. As a beginner, you should perform just *one* exercise per body part. As the weeks turn into months, it may become appropriate to use two exercises for a few of the major body parts, or for areas that are noticeably lagging behind.

The following is a recommended routine for beginners. For the first two workouts, do only one set of each exercise. Afterwards, do the indicated number of sets.

## Beginner's Routine

|  | *Sets* | *Reps* |
|---|---|---|
| Rope Jumping (2 minutes) | | |
| *Shoulders* | | |
| Press behind Neck | 3 × | 10 |
| *Chest* | | |
| Bench Press | 4 × | 8 |
| *Thighs* | | |
| Squat | 3 × | 10 |
| *Back* | | |
| Bent-over Row | 3 × | 10 |
| Prone Hyperextension | 2 × | 15 |

*Mohamed Makkawy performs the crunch exercise for his abdominals.*

Mary Roberts

|  | *Sets* | *Reps* |
|---|---|---|
| *Calves* | | |
| Standing Calf Raise | 3 × | 20 |
| *Triceps* | | |
| Lying Triceps Curl | 3 × | 10 |
| *Biceps* | | |
| Barbell Curl | 3 × | 10 |
| *Forearms* | | |
| Wrist Curl | 3 × | 15 |
| *Abdominals* | | |
| Crunch | 3 × | 15 |

At the beginning stage of bodybuilding, you should not *train heavy*. That is to say, your repetitions should never be below eight in any one set. This is the time when you are finding the groove. (In your initial attempts to lift a weight, the bar will probably wobble. Later, when you find the correct pathway, or groove, you will move the bar in a more controlled manner.)

*Do not* lift heavy poundages at the beginning. Exercise with weights that will allow you to complete a set with no strain. As your experience grows (in six to eight weeks) training with heavier weights will come naturally. When that happens—go for it!

# AEROBIC ROUTINE

Aerobic exercise is almost any exercise performed for 20–40 minutes that is demanding enough to elevate the heart rate and keep it elevated. An aerobic routine can consist of running, jumping, skipping, twisting, arm waving, bouncing, cycling, or rowing. Typically, this type of exercise is performed by groups of people to the beat of loud music at gymnasiums or health clubs. However, thousands of enthusiasts perform aerobic routines in the privacy of their own homes. Before starting an

*Lou Ferrigno rides a bicycle for aerobic exercise.*

*Arnold Schwarzenegger on the run*

aerobic routine, take the following precaution (if it applies to you): men over forty and people with heart problems should have an electrocardiogram taken to make sure that the routine will not overstress the heart.

The basic idea behind aerobic programs is to promote fitness and fat loss. Fair results can be obtained by the performance of two workouts weekly, but it is generally recognized that best advances are made from doing four or five aerobic sessions each week.

The continuous repetition of an exercise elevates your heart rate, however, it should not exceed 80 percent of your maximum heart rate. Subtract your age from 220 to estimate your maximum heart rate. For example, a person who is thirty years old has a maximum heart rate of 190 (220 − 30). Eighty percent of 190 is 152. This person should try to exercise to a point where his or her heart rate is elevated but does not exceed 152. The following chart will help you to find your recommended heart rate during exercise.

| Age | Maximum Heart Rate | 80% of Maximum |
|-----|-----|-----|
| 20 | 200 | 160 |
| 22 | 198 | 158 |
| 24 | 196 | 157 |
| 26 | 194 | 155 |
| 28 | 192 | 154 |
| 30 | 190 | 152 |
| 32 | 189 | 151 |
| 34 | 187 | 150 |
| 36 | 186 | 149 |
| 38 | 184 | 147 |
| 40 | 182 | 146 |
| 45 | 179 | 143 |
| 50 | 175 | 140 |
| 55 | 171 | 137 |
| 60 | 160 | 128 |
| 65 + | 150 | 120 |

## Aerobic Routine*

Stretching (10 minutes)
Stationary Bicycling (10 minutes)
Rope Jumping (5 minutes)
Dancing (to music) (10–15 minutes)
*Do not rest between activities.

# NON-APPARATUS ROUTINE

Although non-apparatus training can be very productive, it does not quite match up to weight training when it comes to building really big muscles and strength. Non-apparatus training puts the exerciser in good condition and muscle tone. When you work with your body weight, rather than with barbell weights, most of the exercises require balance,

*Increased balance is a result of practicing a non-apparatus routine.*

and more muscles are recruited in most movements. Plenty of energy is required, and as a result a higher level of fitness is attained.

To bench press, you must lie securely on a bench in relative comfort. The weight is then handed to you (or taken from racks) to perform the exercise. Only the arms move. In the case of the floor dip, you must begin by balancing on your toes, tensing the abdominals and back, and forcing your head upwards. As you dip up and down, not only the arms and pecs are getting a workout (as in the case of the bench press), but considerably more energy is put into balancing and holding position.

## Non-Apparatus Routine

**Beginner's Workout**

| | Sets | Reps |
|---|---|---|
| *Shoulders* | | |
| Lateral Raise (book in each hand) | 3 × | 15–20 |
| *Thighs* | | |
| Lunge | 3 × | 2 |
| *Calves* | | |
| Calf Raise (feet on stairs) | 3 × | 50 |
| *Chest* | | |
| Floor Dip (3 books under each hand) | 4 × | 25–35 |
| *Back* | | |
| Supine Chin (broomstick across the backs of two chairs) | 4 × | 12–15 |
| *Abdominals* | | |
| Lying Leg Raise (knees bent) | 3 × | 12 |
| *Biceps* | | |
| Self-resistance Curl (curl one arm, resist with the other) | 3 × | 10 |
| *Triceps* | | |
| Reverse Chair Dip (hands on chair behind back, feet straight) | 3 × | 15–20 |

**Advanced Workout**

| | Sets | Reps |
|---|---|---|
| *Shoulders* | | |
| Handstand Dip (against wall) | 3 × | 8 |

Gladys Portugues and Mohamed Makkawy

| | Sets | Reps |
|---|---|---|
| *Thighs* | | |
| Single-leg Squat (from low bench, book under heel) | 3 × | 10 |
| *Calves* | | |
| Single-leg Calf Raise (toes on stairs) | 3 × | 20 |
| *Chest* | | |
| Parallel Dip (between chair backs) | 4 × | 12–15 |
| *Back* | | |
| Chin behind Neck (horizontal bar) | 3 × | 8–12 |
| *Abdominals* | | |
| Crunch (feet on bed or chair) | 3 × | 15 |
| *Biceps* | | |
| Undergrip Chin | 3 × | 10 |
| *Triceps* | | |
| Close-hand Floor Dip (fingers interlocked) | 3 × | 15–20 |

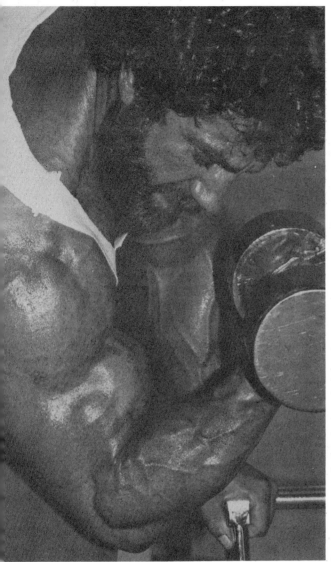

*Jusup Wilkosz demonstrates a dumbbell curl.*

# DUMBBELL ROUTINE

Not everyone has access to a gym. In fact, even today, most people interested in body-building train at home. Many live only in one bedroom apartments with not enough room to hoist a barbell. This results in the individual

having to train with dumbbells. With the exception of being able to perform heavy leg work, dumbbell training can be very beneficial.

Arnold Schwarzenegger favors dumbbell training. He feels that he can "concentrate more when each arm has to do its own reckoning." Frank Zane also performs a lot of dumbbell work, especially when a contest or exhibition is approaching. Writer Tom Smillie, author of the "Advanced Dumbbell Course," which appears in *MuscleMag International*, wrote about dumbbell training superiority:

Dumbbells enable the trainee to attack muscle groups from entirely different angles

*Arnold Schwarzenegger believes that dumbbell training is a highly effective form of bodybuilding.*

than with barbells. Each area performs independently from the other; there is no umbilical cord in the form of a bar linking the weights together. Muscles develop in balance.

Another important aspect of dumbbell training is that the weights tend to find their own pathways, or grooves, whereas a barbell will force your muscles to work in a more fixed pattern. By virtue of this fact—theoretically, at least—dumbbells offer less chance of causing muscle injuries.

## Dumbbell Routine

| | Sets Reps |
|---|---|
| *Shoulders* | |
| Seated Alternate Dumbbell Press | 4 × 8 |
| Lateral Raise | 3 × 10 |
| Bent-over Lateral Raise | 3 × 10 |
| *Thighs* | |
| Squat (heels on block, holding dumbbells at side) | 4 × 20 |
| Sissy Squat (holding dumbbells at sides) | 4 × 15 |
| *Calves* | |
| Single-leg Calf Raise (holding dumbbell) | 4 × 20 |
| *Chest* | |
| Flat Bench Dumbbell Press | 5 × 6–8 |
| Incline Dumbbell Flye | 4 × 10 |
| *Back* | |
| Two-arm Dumbbell Row | 4 × 12 |
| Single-arm Dumbbell Row | 3 × 10 |
| *Abdominals* | |
| Crunch | 3 × 15 |
| *Biceps* | |
| Seated Dumbbell Curl | 4 × 6 |
| Incline Dumbbell Curl | 4 × 8 |
| *Triceps* | |
| Triceps Extension (single dumbbell) | 4 × 8 |
| Lying Dumbbell Triceps Stretch | 4 × 10 |
| *Forearms* | |
| Standing Dumbbell Hammer Curl | 3 × 12 |
| Dumbbell Wrist Curl | 3 × 12 |

*Erika Mes*

# CALVERT ROUTINE

During the first decade of this century, Alan Calvert was the only active exponent of barbell training in America. There was little interest in the sport, except for a few individuals who practiced the bent press, which is a one-arm overhead barbell lift where the torso is bent over parallel to the ground. Then came Alan Calvert's *Strength* magazine, and gradually more barbell exercises were introduced and the popularity of weightlifting grew.

Calvert formulated a standard routine for beginning and intermediate trainers. For all upper body and arm exercises, start with five repetitions. On each third exercise day, add one repetition until you reach ten repetitions. At that time, increase the weight by five pounds, and again perform only five repetitions. For leg exercises, start with ten repetitions, and increase these by two every third workout, until you reach twenty repetitions. Then add ten pounds to the barbell and reduce the repetitions to ten again.

This routine is sound for beginners, but it is important to start with weights well within your capability at the beginning. Training style should be strict. Here are the exercises you can use with this method.

## Calvert Routine

| | Sets | Reps |
|---|---|---|
| *Shoulders* | | |
| Dumbbell Press | 1 | × 5 |
| *Thighs* | | |
| Squat | 1 | × 10 |
| Hack Lift | 1 | × 10 |
| *Chest* | | |
| Bench Press | 1 | × 5 |
| Flat Bench Flye | 1 | × 5 |
| *Back* | | |
| Bent-over Row | 1 | × 5 |
| Deadlift | 1 | × 5 |
| *Trapezius* | | |
| Shrug | 1 | × 5 |
| *Calves* | | |
| Calf Raise | 1 | × 10 |
| *Abdominals* | | |
| Crunch | 1 | × 5 |

# ULTIMATE SHAPING ROUTINE

Every exercise you do works one part of your muscle more than another. Therefore, if you want to build the ultimate shape for your sex, height, bone structure, and genetic inheritance, you should be selective in the exercises you perform.

To simplify an otherwise complicated and frequently debated issue, a generalization of the ideal shape for both men and women can be made. The dynamic and eye-catching physique should have wide shoulders, trim hips, a small waist, arms with balanced development from the wrist to the shoulders, legs that flow aesthetically from the hips to the knees, and then into a full calf development. The lats should be wide, but not too much at the lower lats. The neck should be developed equally on

*Marjo Selin*

*Steve Davis and Heidi Miller combine dramatics and flair in their posing routines.*

# Ultimate Shaping Routine

| | Sets | Reps |
|---|---|---|
| *Thighs* | | |
| Hack Slide | 4 × | 10–12 |
| Thigh Extension | 4 × | 10 |
| Leg Curl | 4 × | 12 |
| *Shoulders* | | |
| Upright Row (wide grip) | 4 × | 8 |
| Lateral Raise | 4 × | 12 |
| Bent-over Lateral Raise | 4 × | 10–12 |
| *Chest* | | |
| Bench Press | 5 × | 8–10 |
| Parallel Bar Dip (wide) | 4 × | 10 |
| *Back* | | |
| Chin behind Neck | 4 × | 10 |
| Seated Pulley Row | 4 × | 12 |
| *Abdominals* | | |
| Hanging Knee Raise | 3 × | 20–25 |
| Crunch | 3 × | 15 |
| *Biceps* | | |
| Incline Dumbbell Curl | 4 × | 8 |
| Preacher Bench Curl (35-degree angle) | 4 × | 10 |
| *Triceps* | | |
| Triceps Pressdown | 4 × | 10 |
| Cradle Bench Rope Pull | 4 × | 10 |
| *Calves* | | |
| Standing Calf Raise | 4 × | 15–20 |
| Donkey Calf Raise | 4 × | 20–25 |

*Mike Christian and Rich Gaspari*

all sides. Pectoral muscles should be built up in all aspects, especially the upper and outer chest region. The glutes should be rounded but not overly heavy in appearance. The overall muscle separation and definition should be clearly visible when contracted or flexed.

The ideal body is exemplified by bodybuilders such as Vince Gironda, Sergio Oliva, Cory Everson, Gladys Portugues, Steve Reeves, and Bob Paris.

Most people do not want huge muscles. On the other hand, Sergio Oliva and Lee Haney have taken the same kind of V-shape development all the way to the Mr. Olympia title. Whether you want 17-inch or 22-inch arms, the training is the same. It's hard.

Here's the ultimate shaping routine that will go a long way towards making you a physical standout on the posing rostrum or a sunny beach.

Ed Kawak, NABBA Mr. Universe

# P.H.A. ROUTINE

P.H.A. (Peripheral Heart Action) training has been in existence for a long time. However, it was in 1966 that it was popularized by Mr. America Bob Gajda. Not only did Bob claim to be able to compress a three-hour workout into one hour, but he also asserted that the method was responsible for his extreme muscularity, which enabled him to beat the famed Sergio Oliva for the Mr. America title.

In regular bodybuilding programs, you work one muscle group at a time, push it to exhaustion, then attack another muscle group. The object is to maintain a constant supply of nutrients and oxygen (carried by the blood) to the muscles. Known as the "muscle pump," this method creates fast gains in size with swollen muscles. By contrast, the P.H.A. system purposely *avoids* the "pump" and provides the benefits of increased circulatory activity. The effect on the heart and lungs is amazing; P.H.A. training is for those who want to maximize their health and physical conditioning.

The regular set system of pumping up is a useful muscle builder that should be utilized by every bodybuilder from time to time. However, to maintain at least a modicum of ruggedness and individual character, the bodybuilder should periodically embark on a different routine. More variety is needed, more attack from different angles.

Many people are under the impression that they should follow the P.H.A. system because it is good for them. This is all very true, but an identical effect on the respiratory organs can be obtained by running for ten minutes. If you jog for an additional fifteen minutes, the benefits can be tripled. P.H.A. training combines circulatory fitness with the muscle-developing effects of weight training.

The method behind a P.H.A. routine is to exercise a muscle group (for example, in the upper body), then immediately do a movement for a completely different body part (the lower body), after which you could do an arm exercise, and then work your waist. Perform one set of each exercise with minimum rest between movements. You should choose four or six exercises to complete one cycle. No two exercises in one cycle should be for the same body part. Perform two or three cycles of each group of exercises. You may take a short breather between each group of exercises, but the general idea is to be constantly in motion until the workout is completed.

## Beginner's P.H.A. Routine
**Cycle I**
Standing Press (Shoulders)
Squat (Thighs)
Chin behind Neck (Back)
Sit-up (Abdominals)
Curl (Biceps)
Heel Raise (Calves)

**Cycle II**
Bench Press (Chest)
Leg Curl (Leg Biceps)
Triceps Extension (Triceps)
Upright Row (Shoulders)
Wrist Curl (Forearms)
Thigh Extension (Thighs)

## Advanced P.H.A. Routine
**Cycle I**
Press behind Neck (Shoulders)
Heel Raise (Calves)
Wide-grip Chin (Back)
Front Squat (Thighs)
Lying Triceps Press (Triceps)
Incline Dumbbell Curl (Biceps)

**Cycle II**
Thigh Extension (Thighs)
Incline Bench Press (Chest)
Crunch (Abdominals)
Seated Calf Raise (Calves)
Wrist Curl (Forearms)
Upright Row (Shoulders)

**Cycle III**
Leg Press (Thighs)
Reverse Curl (Forearms)
Lat Pulldown (Lats)
Flat Bench Flye (Chest)
Single-arm Triceps Extension (Triceps)
Hyperextension (Lower Back)

*Al Beckles works his legs with a thigh extension.*

Mike Mentzer is a Nautilus machine devotee.

# HEAVY-DUTY ROUTINE

It was Mike Mentzer who got people to think about heavy-duty bodybuilding. His articles were read and devoured by ambitious iron pumpers throughout the world. Each article offered common sense and truth. Mentzer

backed up his findings with scientific data that made every iron pumper reach for more weight than ever before. High-intensity determination became the norm in every gym in the country.

Heavy-duty training can be enormously useful, but there are potential pitfalls. One aspect to consider is the possibility of high-intensity effort causing the adrenal glands to

Mohamed Makkawy performs a parallel bar dip, which strongly activates the triceps muscles.

*A lat pulldown . . . Serge Nubret-style*

lose their ability to function. Once a person's adrenals are overloaded, training becomes virtually useless. Energy wanes, strength diminishes, and recuperation is impaired. You feel overtaxed, overfatigued, and overtrained.

Maximum-intensity workouts cannot be practiced effectively for more than three weeks, after which you will have to cut back and do less stressful workouts. Otherwise you will break down, fail to make gains, and even lose muscle size.

Mike Mentzer cautions bodybuilders about overexertion. That is why he recommends a full day's rest after every workout, even if only half the body is trained. Mentzer also feels that the length of high-intensity training should be curtailed sharply, and that forced reps be used only occasionally, perhaps once a week.

## Heavy-Duty Routine

(Note: Perform one warm-up set with about 60 percent of maximum intensity before each exercise.)

| Chest | Sets | Reps |
|---|---|---|
| Pec-Deck Squeeze (to failure) | 2 | × 12 |
| Incline Press (forced reps) | 2 | × 10 |
| Dumbbell Flye | 3 | × 20 |

| Thighs | Sets | Reps |
|---|---|---|
| Thigh Extension | 1 | × 12 |
| Leg Press | 1 | × 10 |
| Back Squat | 1 | × 10 |
| Leg Curl | 1 | × 12 |
| *Deltoids* | | |
| Lateral Raise | 1 | × 12 |
| Seated Barbell Press | 1 | × 10 |
| *Calves* | | |
| Heel Raise (calf machine) | 1 | × 20 |
| Toe Raise (leg-press machine) | 1 | × 20 |
| *Back* | | |
| Pullover (Nautilus machine) | 1 | × 12 |
| Lat Pulldown (to failure) | 1 | × 10 |
| *Biceps* | | |
| Barbell Curl (forced reps) | 1 | × 8 |
| Seated Concentration Curl (to failure) | 1 | × 10 |
| Preacher Bench Curl (90-degree angle) | 1 | × 10 |
| *Triceps* | | |
| Parallel Bar Dip (to failure) | 1 | × 8 |
| Barbell Extension | 1 | × 10 |
| *Abdominals* | | |
| Hanging Leg Raise | 1 | × 20 |
| Crunch | 1 | × 20 |

*Ken-Ichi Suemitsu of Japan*

# PRE-EXHAUST ROUTINE

As mentioned earlier (see page 80), the pre-exhaust system is based on attacking a muscle area, first by exhausting it with an isolation exercise and then immediately performing a combination movement that also involves the target muscle. This method literally forces the isolated muscle to work. It *has* to perform to its limit and thereby additional fibres are brought into play.

It is vital that there is no rest between the isolation movement and the combination movement. Interestingly, even 15–20 seconds of rest will bring about an 80 percent rate of recovery. Those trainers new to pre-exhaustion should limit their sets to two, using something less than maximum poundage for the first couple of workouts. As you get used to this technique, you can work with maximum poundages and increase the number of sets.

## Pre-Exhaust Routine

| | Sets | | Reps |
|---|---|---|---|
| *Shoulders* | | | |
| Lateral Dumbbell Raise | 3 | × | 12 |
| Press behind Neck | 3 | × | 8 |
| *Chest* | | | |
| Flat Bench Flye | 3 | × | 10 |
| Bench Press | 3 | × | 8 |
| *Thighs* | | | |
| Thigh Extension | 3 | × | 12 |
| Squat | 3 | × | 10 |
| *Back* | | | |
| Bent-arm Pullover | 3 | × | 15 |
| T-bar Row | 3 | × | 10 |
| *Abdominals* | | | |
| Crunch | 3 | × | 15 |
| Hanging Leg Raise | 3 | × | 20 |
| *Calves* | | | |
| Standing Calf Raise | 3 | × | 25 |
| Rope Jumping (with weighted handles) | 3 | × | 3 min. |
| *Biceps* | | | |
| Preacher Bench Curl | 3 | × | 12 |
| Narrow Undergrip Chin | 3 | × | 10–15 |
| *Triceps* | | | |
| Triceps Pressdown (lat machine) | 3 | × | 12 |
| Narrow-grip Bench Press | 3 | × | 10 |
| *Forearms* | | | |
| Reverse Wrist Curl | 3 | × | 12 |
| Reverse Curl | 3 | × | 15 |

# OFF-SEASON ROUTINE

Basically, this is a routine to follow when no contests are in sight. It is sometimes known as maintenance training. You are *supposed* to gain on off-season training, but it never gives spectacular results because you are holding back from maximum intensity.

The off-season routine works well with a less restricted diet. However, the number of calories you consume at this time can vary greatly. Depending on sex, age, body weight, and relative *basal metabolic rate* (BMR), you should find a level which allows the muscles to be fully supplied with good nutrition but not so much that the body stores excessive fat reserves.

Your actual training at this time is ruled by moderation. The workouts are usually split in

*Gladys Portugues*

two and training is conducted four or five times a week. Rest periods between exercises are longer than usual—up to one and a half minutes for exercises for the upper body and three minutes for lower body movements.

Supersets and pre-exhaust techniques are seldom incorporated into maintenance workouts, but this isn't mandatory. Although training *performance* is decreased in intensity, workouts at this time often tend to be on the long side to do justice to *all* body parts.

## Off-Season Routine

| | Sets | | Reps |
|---|---|---|---|
| *Chest* | | | |
| Bench Press | 5 | × | 6 |
| Incline Bench Press | 4 | × | 8 |
| Flat Bench Flye | 4 | × | 10 |
| *Thighs* | | | |
| Squat (heels raised) | 5 | × | 6–10 |
| Leg Press (45 degrees) | 4 | × | 10–12 |
| Thigh Curl | 4 | × | 12 |
| *Calves* | | | |
| Standing Calf Raise (machine) | 4 | × | 15–20 |
| Seated Calf Raise (machine) | 4 | × | 15–20 |
| *Shoulders* | | | |
| Seated Press behind Neck | 5 | × | 8 |
| Lateral Dumbbell Raise | 4 | × | 10 |
| Bent-over Lateral Raise | 4 | × | 12 |
| *Back* | | | |
| Wide-grip Chin behind Neck | 4 | × | 10 |
| Lat Pulley (palms parallel to chest) | 4 | × | 10–12 |
| T-bar Row | 4 | × | 10 |
| *Biceps* | | | |
| Barbell Curl | 4 | × | 6 |
| Incline Dumbbell Curl | 4 | × | 8 |
| Preacher Bench Curl (90 degrees) | 4 | × | 10 |
| *Triceps* | | | |
| Close-grip Bench Press | 4 | × | 6–8 |
| Lying Triceps Stretch | 4 | × | 10 |
| Pulley Pushdown | 4 | × | 12 |
| *Abdominals* | | | |
| Roman Chair Sit-up | 3 | × | 25 |
| Hanging Leg Raise | 3 | × | 15 |
| *Forearms* | | | |
| Reverse Curl | 4 | × | 10 |
| Wrist Curl | 4 | × | 12 |

# PRE-CONTEST ROUTINE

Start the pre-contest routine about 12 weeks prior to a competition. As well as gradually tightening your diet, you also intensify your training. As more exercises are added in the final five or six weeks, a concerted effort must be made to reduce the rest time between sets—ultimately to no more than 20–30 seconds. It is common, although not imperative, to use supersets at this time, at least in some exercises which are suitable for it.

Additionally, peak-contraction and continuous-tension reps are advised wherever possible. Use the isotension principle (see page 66). During the final five weeks, you will really be put to the test. Practice your posing on a daily basis (selecting a suitable piece of music to use with your routine), and increase your aerobic exercises. This can take the form of cycling, either on the street or on a stationary bike, jogging, or walking at a brisk pace.

Notice in the pre-contest routine there is a trend towards using isolation exercises. This is necessary to bring out the separation, distinguishing one muscle from another. Use dumbbells and cables in preference to barbells for the same reason. Each body part should be worked three times a week instead of twice, which is normal during off-season training.

## Pre-Contest Routine

| | Sets | Reps |
|---|---|---|
| *Chest* | | |
| Bench Press | 5 × | 8–10 |
| Incline Dumbbell Bench Press | 5 × | 8–10 |
| Flat Bench Flye } superset | 4 × | 10 |
| Cable Crossover | 4 × | 10 |
| *Shoulders* | | |
| Seated Dumbbell Press } superset | 5 × | 8 |
| Seated Dumbbell Lateral Raise | 4 × | 10 |

*Al Beckles, Jusup Wilkosz, and Mohamed Makkawy pose for an unusual picture at a contest.*

| | Sets | Reps |
|---|---|---|
| Bent-over Lateral Raise | 4 × | 12 |
| Alternate Forward Dumbbell Raise | 4 × | 12 |
| *Thighs* | | |
| Hack Lift | 5 × | 10 |
| Thigh Extension | 5 × | 10–15 |
| Lunge | 4 × | 12 |
| Thigh Curl | 5 × | 10–12 |
| *Calves* | | |
| Standing Calf Raise | 4 × | 15–20 |
| Seated Calf Raise | 4 × | 15 |
| Donkey Calf Raise | 4 × | 15–25 |
| *Back* | | |
| Wide-grip Cable Pulldown behind Neck | 4 × | 10 |
| Pulldown to Chest | 4 × | 12 |
| Single-arm Dumbbell Row | 4 × | 10 |
| Seated Cable Row | 4 × | 12 |
| Hyperextension | 4 × | 10–15 |
| *Biceps* | | |
| Incline Dumbbell Curl | 4 × | 10 |

| | Sets | Reps |
|---|---|---|
| Preacher Bench Dumbbell Curl (90 degrees) | 4 × | 8–10 |
| Lying Dumbbell Curl | 4 × | 10 |
| Seated Concentration Curl | 4 × | 12 |
| *Triceps* | | |
| Seated Dumbbell Triceps Stretch | 4 × | 10 |
| Cradle Bench Pulley (face down) | 4 × | 10 |
| Triceps Pressdown | 4 × | 10–12 |
| Bent-over Dumbbell Kickback | 4 × | 8–10 |
| *Abdominals* | | |
| Broomstick Twist | 3 × | 200 |
| Hanging Knee Raise ⎫ superset | 3 × | 20 |
| Crunch ⎭ | 3 × | 20 |
| Lying Half Sit-up | 3 × | 15 |
| *Forearms* | | |
| Reverse Curl ⎫ superset | 5 × | 10–12 |
| Wrist Curl ⎭ | 5 × | 10 |

# POST-EXHAUST ROUTINE

Instead of following an isolation movement with a combination movement, as is the case in the pre-exhaust routine, this method follows a heavy combination (multi-joint) movement with a lighter isolation-type exercise. In other words, the basic muscle fibres are hit first and then a pump is sought with the use of a lighter exercise. This has proven to be one of the most workable methods of all and has been used by virtually all the successful bodybuilders.

## Post-Exhaust Routine

*Billy Arlen*

| | Sets | | Reps |
|---|---|---|---|
| *Chest* | | | |
| Bench Press | 4 | × | 6–10 |
| Flat Bench Flye | 4 | × | 10 |
| *Shoulders* | | | |
| Seated Barbell Press | 4 | × | 6–8 |
| Dumbbell Lateral Raise | 4 | × | 12 |
| *Legs* | | | |
| Front Squat | 4 | × | 6–8 |
| Thigh Extension | 4 | × | 10–12 |
| *Back* | | | |
| T-bar Row | 4 | × | 6–8 |
| Nautilus Pullover | 3 | × | 10–12 |
| *Biceps* | | | |
| Undergrip Chin | 4 | × | 8 |
| Seated Concentration Curl | 4 | × | 10 |
| *Triceps* | | | |
| Close-grip Bench Press | 4 | × | 6–8 |
| Triceps Pulley Pressdown | 4 | × | 10–12 |
| *Abdominals* | | | |
| Hanging Leg Raise | 4 | × | 15 |
| Crunch | 4 | × | 15 |
| *Calves* | | | |
| Standing Calf Raise | 4 | × | 15–20 |
| Toe Raise (leg-press machine) | 4 | × | 20–25 |

# ONE-EXERCISE-PER-BODY-PART ROUTINE

When asked about the best length for a workout, trainer Vince Gironda said:

I am a great believer in short workouts, training 85–90 percent intensity, using only one exercise per body part. If you want size, this is a great method to achieve it!

The beauty of the one-exercise-per-body-part routine is its simplicity. If you are used to exercising with three or four exercises per body part, you may find yourself putting 100 percent more effort and concentration into your training when doing one exercise per body part.

The exercises selected in this routine are movements that work the *belly* of the muscle. There would be little point in doing exercises that develop only the upper or lower sections of a muscle group. It is important to do exercises that develop the major portions of the muscles.

## One-Exercise-Per-Body-Part Routine

|  | Sets | Reps |
|---|---|---|
| *Chest* | | |
| Medium-grip Bench Press | 8 × | 8 |
| *Shoulders* | | |
| Seated Dumbbell Press (elbows out) | 8 × | 8 |
| *Thighs* | | |
| Parallel Squat (heels on blocks) | 8 × | 6–10 |
| *Calves* | | |
| Donkey Calf Raise (feet parallel) | 8 × | 15–20 |
| *Back* | | |
| Medium-grip Chin to Chest | 8 × | 10 |
| *Biceps* | | |
| Incline Dumbbell Curl | 8 × | 8 |
| *Triceps* | | |
| Close-grip Parallel Bar Dip | 8 × | 8 |
| *Abdominals* | | |
| Hanging Knee Raise | 5 × | 15–20 |

*Gladys Portugues struggles with an upright row.*

# BEAT-THE-CLOCK ROUTINE

You have only so much time to train. Sure you want to be fit. You want a great body, but time is scarce. Do you have 20 minutes, three days a week? That's all it takes for this routine.

Most of the exercises in this time-efficient schedule are actually two exercises in one! Be prepared, though—what you save in time you will spend in effort. And your cardiovascular system will benefit enormously.

## Beat-the-Clock Routine

|  | Sets | Reps |
|---|---|---|
| Rope Jumping (3 minutes) | | |
| *Shoulders, Arms, Back* | | |
| Barbell Clean and Press | 1 × | 12–15 |
| *Chest, Arms, Back* | | |
| Bent-arm Pullover/Bench Press | 1 × | 10–12 |
| *Lower Back and Shoulders* | | |
| Stiff-legged Deadlift/Upright Row | 1 × | 10 |
| *Shoulders, Back, Thighs* | | |
| Squat Clean and Jerk | 1 × | 10 |
| *Biceps* | | |
| Barbell Curl | 2 × | 12 |
| *Triceps* | | |
| Triceps Stretch | 2 × | 12 |
| *Abdominals* | | |
| Hanging Leg Raise | 1 × | 15 |
| Crunch | 1 × | 20 |

*Posing sensation John Brown of California*

# BULK ROUTINE

Many athletes require extra body weight for their sports. If you're a skinny bodybuilder having difficulty putting on the pounds, the bulk routine may be useful to you. You should be warned, however, that bulking up for the bodybuilder who already has some muscles is not the greatest idea. Many well-developed men with 17–18-inch arms have totally ruined their physiques by falling for the bulk craze, and adding an extra 20–30 pounds.

To gain weight, you must eat substantial amounts of food and exercise moderately. Eat plenty of poultry, fish, fruit, vegetables, cheese, eggs, yogurt, and above all—drink milk. Try to eat six smaller meals each day rather than two or three bigger ones. Your bulk routine is not long and should be practiced only two or three times a week. You may even use it on a four-day split if you wish (working each body part twice weekly).

## Bulk Routine

| Chest and Triceps | Sets | Reps |
|---|---|---|
| Bench Press | 1 | × 10 |
| | 3 | × 3 |
| | 2 | × 10 |
| **Legs and Lower Back** | | |
| Squat | 1 | × 12 |
| | 3 | × 3 |
| | 2 | × 12 |
| **Shoulders and Triceps** | | |
| Press behind Neck | 1 | × 10 |
| | 3 | × 4 |
| | 2 | × 10 |
| **Back and Arms** | | |
| Bent-over Row | 1 | × 12 |
| | 3 | × 5 |
| | 2 | × 10 |
| **Biceps** | | |
| Barbell Curl | 1 | × 12 |
| | 3 | × 6 |
| | 1 | × 12 |

# NATURAL BODYBUILDER'S ROUTINE

There's certainly something to be said for natural bodybuilding. This is to say, weight training for men and women without the use of drugs (anabolic steroids).

Steroids in all their forms *do* help the bodybuilder recuperate faster. They allow a person to train longer, with more zest and determination; they even make for a better pump. However, steroid use can cause severe liver damage, even cancer, and high-blood pressure, and they may predispose you to heart and circulatory problems in later life.

Gary Leonard and Kay Baxter

Apart from the fact that steroid abuse can cause irreparable damage to your body, they tend to bloat the physique. Although I have never taken a steroid in my life, I have known many bodybuilders who have. I have seen the steroid "high" (that moment when the body reacts to the drug and extra size and strength seems to come overnight), and I have seen the "low" periods (shrivelled muscles, weakness, and hospitalization).

Natural training is best. By doing the right exercises and eating wholesome foods, you can stimulate all the hormone production required.

*Dick Baldwin*

*John Terilli*

# Natural Bodybuilder's Routine

|  | Sets | Reps |
|---|---|---|
| *Shoulders* | | |
| Standing Barbell Press | 4 × | 6–8 |
| Lateral Raise | 3 × | 10 |
| Bent-over Flye | 4 × | 12 |
| *Legs* | | |
| Front Squat | 4 × | 8–10 |
| Hack Slide | 3 × | 12 |
| Thigh Curl | 3 × | 12 |
| *Calves* | | |
| Standing Calf Raise | 4 × | 15–20 |
| *Chest* | | |
| Dumbbell Bench Press | 4 × | 8 |
| Incline Flye | 4 × | 10 |
| Straight-arm Pullover | 3 × | 12 |
| *Back* | | |
| Wide-grip Chin | 4 × | 8–12 |
| Single-arm Dumbbell Row | 3 × | 12 |
| *Abdominals* | | |
| Knee Raise (on flat bench) | 4 × | 20 |
| *Biceps* | | |
| Close-grip Barbell Curl | 4 × | 10 |
| Alternate Dumbbell Curl | 4 × | 8 |
| *Triceps* | | |
| Parallel Bar Dip | 4 × | 8 |
| Lying Triceps Stretch | 4 × | 10 |

# CIRCUIT-TRAINING ROUTINE

The circuit-training method requires setting up 12–15 exercise stations around the gym with exercises for all the muscle groups. As a general rule, do not perform two exercises in a row for the same muscle area. Commence the routine by moving from station to station, with no more than 15 seconds of rest between exercises.

Several circuits (up to five) may be used during a precontest training cycle. It is a good idea to use a high degree of intensity when training with this method, which ensures that muscle mass is kept to a maximum even though you are burning calories to reduce fat levels. Do not perform circuit training as a way

*Kris Alexander*

*Look at the incredible biceps of Deanna Panting.*

to prepare for a contest condition unless you feel comfortable with it. The method is different from most others and just may not suit you mentally or physically. Try it out during the off season before choosing it for your precontest preparation. The following is a sample schedule.

## Circuit-Training Routine

| | Sets | Reps |
|---|---|---|
| Standing Barbell Press (Shoulders) | 1 | × 12 |
| Hyperextension (Lower Back) | 1 | × 12 |
| Calf Raise (Calves) | 1 | × 25 |
| Bench Press (Chest) | 1 | × 10 |
| Wrist Curl (Forearms) | 1 | × 12 |
| Thigh Curl (Legs) | 1 | × 12 |
| Parallel Bar Dip (Triceps) | 1 | × 10 |
| Crunch (Abdominals) | 1 | × 15 |
| Leg Extension (Thighs) | 1 | × 12 |
| Barbell Curl (Biceps) | 1 | × 10 |
| Seated Pulley Row (Back) | 1 | × 10 |
| Flat Bench Flye (Chest) | 1 | × 10 |
| Squat (Legs) | 1 | × 8 |
| Triceps Extension (Triceps) | 1 | × 10 |
| Lateral Raise (Shoulders) | 1 | × 10 |

*Sergio Oliva shows his massive arms in a parallel bar dip.*

# POTPOURRI ROUTINE

This method is even older than the set system. John Grimek used it 50 years ago, with great results. In potpourri training, you perform up to six or even more exercises per body part, but only one set for each exercise.

Vary the amount of repetitions used in each exercise to suit your needs. In some exercises you may want to work heavy using 5–8 reps; in others you may feel the urge to really blast away to complete a set of 12 or even more reps.

"I like exercise variety," said Sergio Oliva, who has worked with a similar program to add variety to his exercise regimen. "Exercise monotony is a major cause of progress standstill. You need constant variety to maintain mental interest and physical freshness."

The great advantage of potpourri training is that you have enormous variety and are consequently hitting each muscle group from different angles. Bodybuilder Don Ross suggested:

> In keeping with the spirit of variety, you should utilize *different* repetitions on each exercise, using heavy weights and low repetitions on some and lighter weights and higher reps on others.

# Potpourri Routine

| *Shoulders and Trapezius* | Sets | Reps |
|---|---|---|
| Seated Front Press | 1 × | 5 |
| Wide-grip Upright Row | 1 × | 8 |
| Seated Press behind Neck | 1 × | 10 |
| Lateral Raise | 1 × | 12 |
| Alternate Front Dumbbell Raise | 1 × | 10 |
| Standing Dumbbell Press | 1 × | 8 |
| High Pull (Smith machine) | 1 × | 6 |
| Dumbbell Shrug | 1 × | 8 |

| *Upper Back and Rear Deltoids* | Sets | Reps |
|---|---|---|
| Wide-grip Chin behind Head | 1 × | 10 |
| Bent-over Row | 1 × | 8 |
| Pulldown to Chest | 1 × | 12 |
| Wide-grip Pulldown behind Head | 1 × | 12 |
| T-bar Row | 1 × | 8 |
| Bent-arm Pullover | 1 × | 12 |
| Seated Cable Row | 1 × | 12 |
| Single-arm Dumbbell Row | 1 × | 5 |

| *Lower Back and Waist* | Sets | Reps |
|---|---|---|
| Prone Hyperextension | 1 × | 15 |
| Crunch | 1 × | 20 |
| Side Bend (single dumbbell) | 1 × | 25 |
| Stiff-legged Deadlift | 1 × | 15 |
| Good-Morning Exercise | 1 × | 15 |
| Hanging Leg Raise | 1 × | 15 |
| Seated Knee Raise | 1 × | 20 |

| *Chest* | Sets | Reps |
|---|---|---|
| Bench Press | 1 × | 6 |
| Incline Bench Press | 1 × | 8 |
| Flat Bench Flye | 1 × | 10 |
| Cable Crossover | 1 × | 15 |
| Incline Bench Flye | 1 × | 10 |
| Decline Dumbbell Bench Press | 1 × | 6 |
| Straight-arm Pullover | 1 × | 15 |
| Wide-grip Parallel Bar Dip | 1 × | 12 |

The mighty back of Sergio Oliva

| *Triceps* | Sets | Reps |
|---|---|---|
| Single-dumbbell Triceps Press (with both hands) | 1 × | 12 |
| Dumbbell Triceps Kickback | 1 × | 10 |
| Parallel Bar Dip | 1 × | 6 |
| Triceps Pully Pressdown | 1 × | 12 |
| Close-grip Bench Press | 1 × | 8 |
| Lying Triceps Stretch | 1 × | 10 |
| Standing Barbell Triceps Stretch | 1 × | 6 |

| *Biceps* | Sets | Reps |
|---|---|---|
| Preacher Bench Curl (90 degrees) | 1 × | 10 |
| Barbell Curl | 1 × | 6 |

*(continued on next page)*

| | Sets | Reps |
|---|---|---|
| Incline Dumbbell Curl | 1 × | 10 |
| Preacher Bench Curl (35 degrees) | 1 × | 12 |
| Lat-machine Curl (lying on bench) | 1 × | 20 |
| Concentration Curl | 1 × | 10 |
| Undergrip Chin | 1 × | 6 |
| *Forearms* | | |
| Wrist Curl (dumbbells) | 1 × | 15 |
| Reverse Wrist Curl (barbell) | 1 × | 15 |
| Preacher Bench Hammer Curl (thumbs up) | 1 × | 12 |
| Reverse Barbell Curl | 1 × | 10 |
| Wrist Curl (barbell behind thighs) | 1 × | 20 |
| *Thighs* | | |
| Leg Press | 1 × | 6 |
| Standing Leg Curl | 1 × | 10 |
| Front Squat | 1 × | 5 |
| Hack Lift | 1 × | 10 |
| Leg Extension | 1 × | 12 |
| Smith Machine Squat | 1 × | 10 |
| Lying Leg Curl | 1 × | 15 |
| *Calves* | | |
| Calf Raise (full stretch with no weight) | 1 × | 30–50 |
| Standing Calf Raise (machine) | 1 × | 20 |
| Seated Calf Raise | 1 × | 15 |
| Calf Raise (leg-press machine) | | |
| Calf Raise (hack machine) | 1 × | 20 |
| Donkey Calf Raise | 1 × | 25 |

# INJURED-BACK ROUTINE

It's not just bodybuilders who injure their backs. It happens to everyone sooner or later. If you pull a muscle or otherwise strain your lower back, you will need to rest it. Stop whatever you did to cause the pain. If the pain is severe and you also have it in the leg, this is

*Note the terrific definition in Frank Zane's back.*

probably due to the nerves being pinched by a collapsed disc in the spinal column. An overweight or heavily muscled body can make any backache worse because of the additional weight. One of the main problems with backaches is that they don't always clear up quickly or completely. If the strain does not ease quickly, see your doctor.

Bad or weak backs are so common that bodybuilders suffering from weakened back conditions have to work around the injury whenever training is undertaken. Exercises that can cause lower back problems include: bent-over barbell rowing, heavy seated concentration curls, squats, and deadlifts, performed in poor style. Remember, if your back gives you sharp pains that do not clear up, or if you have a constant dull ache in the area, then see your doctor.

## Injured-Back Routine

| | Sets | Reps |
|---|---|---|
| *Shoulders* | | |
| Seated Dumbbell Upright Row | 4 × | 12 |
| Seated Lateral Raise | 3 × | 10 |

*Lori Bowen-Rice*

| Chest | Sets Reps |
|---|---|
| Bench Press | 4 × 6–8 |
| Supine Flye | 3 × 10 |
| *Thighs* | |
| Leg Press (45 degrees with light weight) | 2 × 15 |
| Hack Slide | 3 × 12 |
| Thigh Extension | 3 × 12 |
| Thigh Curl | 3 × 15 |
| *Calves* | |
| Seated Calf Raise | 4 × 20 |
| *Back* | |
| Chin behind Neck | 4 × 10 |
| Close-grip Pulldown | 3 × 12 |
| Hyperextension | 2 × 15 |
| *Biceps* | |
| Incline Dumbbell Curl | 4 × 10 |
| Seated Alternate Dumbbell Curl | 3 × 12 |
| *Triceps* | |
| Close-grip Bench Press | 4 × 8 |
| Triceps Pressdown | 3 × 15 |
| *Abdominals* | |
| Hanging Knee Raise | 3 × 15–20 |

# EXECUTIVE'S ROUTINE

Most business executives today carry a briefcase. This is the symbol of success and also a symbol of stress. A briefcase is another way of saying that you *don't* leave your work at the office.

In spite of all this, business people should be aware that fitness pays off in the board room. According to statistics, the fitter a person is the better he or she is able to handle stress, which makes for better business performance. Although there are some pretty poor physical specimens among the wealthy people of the world, the common image now among corporate directors, executives, and managers is typically that of a very fit, strong, and energetic person.

Naturally, few businessmen have the time or the inclination to build a Mr. Universe-type physique, but there is still the desire to possess a well-shaped body. The following routine is relatively brief but effective. It will serve to bring you both fitness and an attractive physique. Perform it three times weekly, although you could get by with only two training sessions if time is scarce.

## Executive's Routine

| | Sets Reps |
|---|---|
| *Warm-up* | |
| Rope Jumping (3 minutes) | |
| *Chest* | |
| Medium-grip Bench Press | 3 × 15 |
| *Thighs* | |
| Hack Lift (hold barbell behind legs, with heels on block) | 2 × 12–15 |
| *Calves* | |
| Standing Calf Raise (barbell across shoulders) | 2 × 15 |

*(continued on next page)*

Gladys Portugues and trainer Ken Wheeler

| Shoulders | Sets | Reps |
|---|---|---|
| Alternate Seated Dumbbell Press | 2 × | 15 |
| Back | | |
| Bent-over Row (barbell to waist) | 2 × | 15 |
| Biceps | | |
| Barbell Curl | 2 × | 15 |
| Triceps | | |
| Barbell Triceps Stretch | 2 × | 15 |
| Abdominals | | |
| Seated Knee Raise | 1 × | 50 |
| Broomstick Twist | 1 × | 200 |
| Cardiovascular | | |
| Rope Jumping (2 sets of 3–4 minutes each) | | |

# TENDON-BUILDING ROUTINE

Building great tendon strength takes special training techniques. Strong ligaments and tendons are inherited factors, but you can improve tendon strength by the way in which you train. A tendon is a tough, fibrous tissue joining muscle to bone, whereas a ligament is the attachment joining one bone to another. Muscle size alone—although it goes hand in hand with strength—is not the most important ingredient for super power. Your ligament and tendon strength is the important factor.

It should also be borne in mind that bodybuilders who spend time strengthening their tendons and ligaments can put that strength to use in their regular bodybuilding program. In short, you will be able to use more weight in your other exercises. Many who have gone on a specific tendon-strengthening course for a six-to-eight-week period have been able to increase their poundages on virtually all exercises. And that means larger muscles will be the result.

It is generally accepted that weight training with a high number of sets and reps may burn up excessive tissue and energy that can leave you feeling debilitated or overtired. However, heavy tendon training does not break down massive amounts of tissue, making it possible for the body to handle the rebuilding job with greater ease. Many fitness and health experts favor tendon training rather than long-drawn-out conventional bodybuilding workouts.

Tendon training is always maximized if you feed your muscles with the best possible nutrients. Soft, weak tendons may be aided by the addition of manganese tablets (50 mg) to your diet program. Fred Howell, the champion of tendon and ligament training, prepares a special drink that he relies on to get him through the day with energy to spare. This is his recipe: Take a large glass of unsweetened grape juice, thin it with a quarter cup of water, then add four tablespoons of liquid protein and two teaspoons of a B-vitamin/iron supplement. Howell also advises that serious trainers take some wheat-germ oil and a vitamin E tablet.

If you are new to tendon training, you must start slowly. Begin with light weights and be content to make progress at a moderate rate. Give yourself two or three weeks before you increase your workout intensity. The tendons and ligaments need this time to get used to the exercises and gain the necessary coordination. It may take some experimentation to find the exercises that best suit your body. Bear in

*Lori Bowen-Rice*

*Steve Davis*

mind that you may experience "surge training." That is to say, you may suddenly find that your strength increases dramatically. It *can* happen only with this type of training.

When you experience surge training you will suddenly find that your usual training poundage feels light. You will enthusiastically add ten or twenty pounds to the bar. Make the most of it. You won't have too many miracle days like this. At first, you may not even believe it. You'll count up the discs to make sure you haven't made an error. With tendon training, you may never be restricted by your usual poundages again.

*Cammie Lusko uses superheavy poundage for the six-inch squat.*

# Tendon-Building Routine

**Hyperextension (Lower Back)**    On a hyperextension bench, perform three sets of ten repetitions. Add weight by holding loose discs behind your neck when you increase strength in your lower back. As an alternative to a hyperextension bench, you may use a high table with a partner holding down your feet on one end. Make sure he or she holds them securely, especially if you are using weight.

**Six-Inch Squat (Knees, Lower Back, Thighs)**    There is no substitute for either squat stands or power racks for this exercise.

The last thing you want to worry about is whether or not the bar is properly supported. There must be no possibility of missing the stands when you perform this heavy lift. The point to remember is that the stands must be directly below the loaded barbell at all times.

With the bar about six inches lower than your shoulders on the rack, load up a substantial weight. Get under the bar with your back straight and knees bent. Then, by straightening your knees, lift the weight off the rack, relax, bend the knees a few inches, and straighten your legs again. Perform five sets of five reps. Increase the weight when you feel able to handle it.

**Supine Press Lockout (Chest, Arms, Shoulders, Wrists, Elbows)** Arrange your loaded barbell on two sturdy boxes so that when you're lying on your back, under the weight, you will have a 6–8-inch distance to press. For back comfort, you should have a mat of some kind. Take a comfortable, fairly wide grip on the bar and press up until the elbows lock. Perform four sets of four reps. Make sure that the boxes are not only adequately strong to support the entire weight, but also prevent the barbell from rolling off the supports. Nail two additional pieces of wood on each box to prevent the barbell from rolling off the supports. After a few weeks with this exercise, your regular bench press will feel as light as a feather.

**Partial Deadlift (Lower Back, Forearms, Upper Back)** Arrange a heavy barbell on strong boxes at a height whereby you can commence a partial deadlift from 4–6 inches above your bent knees to the straight-legged position. Keep your back straight, head to the front, one palm facing forward, the other in the opposite position. Do not round your back as you lift upwards. Lower and repeat. Do four sets of four reps. Do not jerk the weight from the boxes. Do not rely on any grip aids, such as straps, in the exercise. You can, of course, use chalk powder to eliminate any slipping possibility, which may result from sweaty hands.

**Partial Row (Forearms, Shoulders, Biceps, Back)** Lift a heavy barbell from your boxes (as in the previous deadlift exercise) and stand erect, holding the bar in front of your upper thighs as you begin the rowing exercise. In actuality, raise the bar no more than 6–8 inches in front of you. Then lower the bar to the starting position. Aim for four sets of four repetitions.

Combine the above tendon-building routine with a ten-minute run or jog twice a week, in conjunction with a couple of sets of abdominal crunches or knee raises. Perform no other supplementary movements, even though you may be accustomed to performing many different exercises in your routine. Neither is it a good idea to train more than three days a week. In fact, some people find that they get best results from using this schedule only two times weekly (with a two-day rest between workouts).

Start this type of exercise cautiously. Do not lift weights that are excessively heavy at first. Remember that your first two sets are warm-up sets. Sturdy equipment is the secret of supreme confidence and that is the ingredient that will lead you to supreme success.

Powerful tendons and ligaments will be the result if you follow this routine.

*Ernie Santiago*

# POWER SQUAT ROUTINE

Fred Hatfield, Ph.D., has some very potent words to say about the squat exercise:

The squat, more than any other movement in weight training, has been misunderstood, banned, maligned, performed improperly, and surrounded with the most incredible old wives' tales possible to imagine.

*Is it possible? Sam Sanchez gives it a try.*

There is confusion regarding the squat exercise. Not just bodybuilders, but exercise physiologists, coaches, and doctors have a diversity of ideas and theories that conflict with one another. When I first trained in France 20 years ago, I was shocked to find that no one did squats. The only leg exercises performed were hack lifts and thigh extensions. They believed it was bad for the heart. Today in North America no one blames heart trouble on squats, but we do get the "bad for the knees" comments and, "Squats will slow you down and rob you of flexibility." And finally, "Squats will give you a broad butt." Actually, there is a grain of truth in all these statements, as I will explain.

**Squats and the Heart**    A healthy heart will *not* be damaged by heavy squatting or any other vigorous exercise. However, if an individual has a congenital heart problem, high-blood pressure, angina, or other circulatory heart problems, then heavy squats (or heavy exercise of any kind) could precipitate problems.

**Squats and the Knees**    Some people have stronger ligaments and knee joints than others. It doesn't take a genius to figure out that the knee and its surrounding connective tissues take a great deal of strain during the motion of squatting with a heavy barbell across the back. To avoid knee problems:

1. Warm up the knee joints carefully before piling on the weights. Do thigh extensions, free squats, and gradually increase the poundage. Several sets of squats are required before maximum weights are used.
2. Squat down only until the thighs are parallel to the floor. Some trainers, however, prefer to go all the way. The important thing is that you go down slowly. Never bounce out of the low position, which will definitely injure the knees.

**Speed and Flexibility**    Squats will not interfere with the "speed" of your muscles. In fact, they will tune up your legs and *prepare* them for speed. Remember, however, that we are only good at what we practice. If an Olympic runner were to give up running, then he would lose his speed. You will lose whatever you don't practice. Many of the world's fastest runners do heavy squats.

The same goes for flexibility. If you do not keep up your flexibility movements, you will gradually lose the skill. Tom Platz, possessor of the world's most muscular thighs, is amazingly flexible, because he keeps at his stretching exercises.

**Squats and Butt Size**    Butt size is governed by your hip size (the width of your pelvic structure). If you do really heavy, flat-footed squats, leaning forward excessively, coming out of the squat backside first, head between the knees, you can widen the glutes

*Tom Platz has the world's most muscular thighs.*

and build unaesthetic muscles on the upper glute area. On the other hand, if you avoid all heavy squat exercises, your glutes will be flat and have no muscle roundness at all. The glutes are muscles that should be developed in balanced proportion to the rest of the body.

Heavy squats are unbelievably hard work. Yet the squat is popular among top bodybuilders because it is openly recognized as the king of all exercises. You must use squat racks to do the exercise properly. When going for heavy low reps you must also train with two workout partners, or else have special "catchers" built alongside your squat racks. It is no fun at all being caught in the *down* position with a few hundred pounds on your back. Always wear a strong lifting belt.

Generally speaking, powerlifters take a wider stance than bodybuilders. They also tend to lean forward more as they rise up out of a squat, with the chest closer to the knees. The bodybuilder should use a more upright stance, with head up, hips under the bar, and the back flat and erect as possible. The bar should rest across the trapezius muscle and the weight should be distributed evenly along the feet.

Breathe in deeply just before lowering into the squat; exhale as the knees lock out at the completion of each rep. Always end a power squat routine with exercises for the other major body parts—shoulders, chest, back, arms, etc.

## Beginner's Power Squat Routine*

|  | Sets | Reps |
|---|---|---|
| Free-standing Squat (no weight) | 1 × 20 | |
| Squat (with weight) | 1 × 12 | |
|  | 1 × 8 | |
|  | 2 × 4 | |
|  | 2 × 2 | |

*To be followed three days a week. Try to increase weights every third workout. You can try a single best "limit" squat once every two or three weeks.

## Advanced Power Squat Routine**

|  | Sets | Reps |
|---|---|---|
| Free-standing Squat (no weight) | 1 × 15 | |
| Squat (with weight) | 1 × 12–15 | |
|  | 1 × 8 | |
|  | 1 × 6 | |
|  | 1 × 4 | |
|  | 1 × 3 | |
|  | 1 × 2 | |
|  | 1 × 2 | |

**Only go for a maximum "limit" squat once a month. Rest up to five minutes between heavy sets.

Dave Spector

# MUSCLE-SPINNING ROUTINE

Muscle spinning was the training method first used in the 1950s by California bodybuilders who gained size and muscle shape without bothering to develop strength. They were cosmetic bodybuilders with no interest in what poundage they could lift. Today the muscle-spinning system may not be ideal to train with all year round (although some bodybuilders do), but it could help you to overcome

Ed Corney

fullest muscle pump. The whole muscle-spinning technique is dependent on keeping the muscles flushed and pumped from one day to the next. Exercise each muscle area no less than three times weekly.

## Muscle-Spinning Routine

| | Sets | Reps |
|---|---|---|
| *Shoulders* | | |
| Seated Dumbbell Press | 5 | × 15 |
| Upright Row | 5 | × 15 |
| Lateral Raise | 5 | × 15 |
| Bent-over Flye | 5 | × 15 |
| *Thighs* | | |
| Front Squat | 5 | × 25 |
| Hack Lift | 5 | × 25 |
| Thigh Extension | 5 | × 25 |
| Thigh Curl | 5 | × 25 |
| *Chest* | | |
| Bench Press | 5 | × 15 |
| Incline Bench Press | 5 | × 15 |
| Lying Flye | 5 | × 15 |
| Decline Flye | 5 | × 15 |
| *Upper Back and Traps* | | |
| Wide-grip Pulldown | 5 | × 15 |
| Close-grip Pulldown | 5 | × 15 |
| High Bench Row | 5 | × 15 |
| Seated Cable Row | 5 | × 15 |
| *Biceps* | | |
| Preacher Curl (45 degrees) | 5 | × 15 |
| High Bench Dumbbell Curl | 5 | × 15 |
| Alternate Seated Dumbbell Curl | 5 | × 15 |
| *Triceps* | | |
| Lying Triceps Stretch | 5 | × 15 |
| Two-arm Triceps Stretch (with one dumbbell) | 5 | × 15 |
| Lying Dumbbell Triceps Stretch | 5 | × 15 |
| *Abdominals and Lower Back* | | |
| Hanging Knee Raise | 5 | × 25 |
| Prone Hyperextension | 5 | × 15 |
| Crunch | 5 | × 25 |
| Side Bend (with one dumbbell) | 5 | × 25 |
| *Forearms* | | |
| Seated Barbell Wrist Curl | 5 | × 25 |
| Seated Barbell Reverse Wrist Curl | 5 | × 25 |
| Reverse Curl | 5 | × 25 |

a sticking point if practiced for 8–12 weeks of the year.

The muscle-spinning routine is the exact opposite of the heavy-duty routine. If you use this method after heavy-duty training, you will not notice any new muscle gains immediately. However, after a few weeks, your muscles should gain some size.

The basic rules for the muscle-spinning routine are to perform three or four exercises per body part, five sets per exercise, working 15 repetitions when training torso and upper arms, and 25 reps when training legs, forearms, and abdominals. Use only light to moderate weights. Do not perform forced reps. Your exercise style should be strict at all times, performing the repetitions briskly. Reduce rest periods between exercises as much as possible. Split the routine in two, training six days a week. Concentrate on obtaining the

*Mike Christian*

# NAUTILUS ROUTINE

In 1970, after 20 years of experiments, Arthur Jones built and sold an exercise machine. It was a pullover apparatus for the torso—the first machine on the market to provide full-range variable resistance. Jones went on to invent many more machines, which were advertised in *Iron Man* magazine. He also wrote a series of training manuals, which said: Do high-intensity exercise that lasts between 30–70 seconds. Practice slow repetitions. (Research undertaken at Nautilus labs over the last 15 years indicates that for bodybuilding, slow repetitions are far more productive than fast ones.) As a general rule, each repetition should take approximately six seconds to perform (two seconds to lift the weight, four seconds to lower it).

According to Jones, exercise performance must be continued until positive muscle failure takes place, and non-involved muscles should be relaxed as much as possible during each exercise. The negative aspect (return of the weight to starting position) should be accentuated whenever possible. The number of sets and reps is an estimate, which you should tailor to your body. Arthur Jones incorporated the pre-exhaust system into his training philosophy since he saw it as a way to increase intensity to a targeted muscle.

## Men's Nautilus Routine

| | Sets | | Reps |
|---|---|---|---|
| *Back* | | | |
| Hip and Back Machine | 1–2 | × | 8–15 |
| Torso Row | 1–2 | × | 8–15 |
| *Thighs* | | | |
| Leg Extension | 1–2 | × | 8–15 |
| Leg Press | 1–2 | × | 8–15 |
| *Shoulders* | | | |
| Lateral Raise (Double Shoulder Machine) | 1–2 | × | 8–15 |

*(continued on page 128)*

*Brian Homka gives Scott Wilson a helping hand on the Nautilus machine.*

| Chest | Sets | | Reps |
|---|---|---|---|
| Pullover | 1–2 | × | 8–15 |
| Chest Machine | 1–2 | × | 8–15 |
| Incline Press | 1–2 | × | 8–15 |
| *Triceps* | | | |
| Multi-exercise Triceps Dip | 1–2 | × | 8–15 |
| *Biceps* | | | |
| Biceps Curl (negative emphasis) | 1–2 | × | 8–15 |
| *Calves* | | | |
| Multi-exercise Calf Negative | 1–2 | × | 8–15 |
| *Forearms* | | | |
| Multi-exercise Wrist Curl | 1–2 | × | 8–15 |

# Women's Nautilus Routine

| Back | Sets | | Reps |
|---|---|---|---|
| Hip and Back Machine | 1–2 | × | 8–15 |

| Thighs | Sets | | Reps |
|---|---|---|---|
| Leg Extension | 1–2 | × | 8–15 |
| Leg Press | 1–2 | × | 8–15 |
| *Chest* | | | |
| Pullover | 1–2 | × | 8–15 |
| Arm Cross (Double Chest or Women's Chest Machine) | 1–2 | × | 8–15 |
| Incline Press (Double Chest Machine) | 1–2 | × | 8–15 |
| *Shoulders* | | | |
| Lateral Raise (Double Shoulder Machine) | 1–2 | × | 8–15 |
| Overhead Press (negative movement if weight cannot be pressed five times) | 1–2 | × | 8–15 |
| *Arms* | | | |
| Torso-Arm Machine | 1–2 | × | 8–15 |
| Biceps Curl | 1–2 | × | 8–15 |
| Multi-exercise Wrist Curl | 1–2 | × | 8–15 |
| *Calves* | | | |
| Multi-exercise Calf Raise | 1–2 | × | 8–15 |

*Kiki Elomaa performs a leg extension on a machine.*

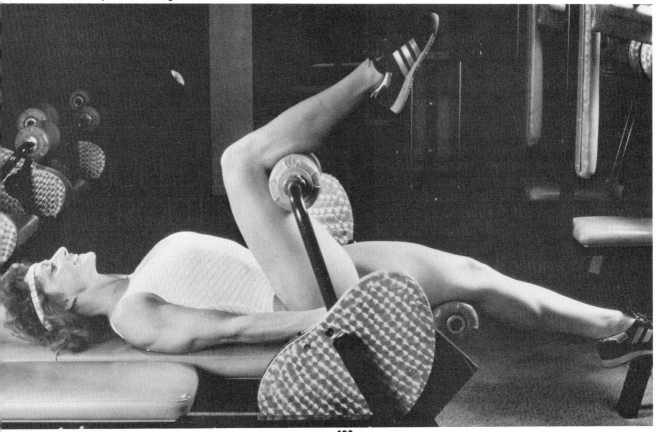

# MASS-BUILDING ROUTINE

Mass building is obtained through the performance of basic, multi-joint training. These basic exercises are the ones which work more than one of the large muscle groups at a time with heavy weights.

Bodybuilders often periodically go on mass-building routines. Men like Roy Callender have spent long periods training with mass-building programs. Today he does at least one such workout each week.

Pyramiding the weight (adding poundage after each set) works well with this type of schedule. In fact, most experienced bodybuilders pyramid their poundages when working with heavy weights and multi-joint exercises. The advanced bodybuilder requires more and more warm-up sets as his or her body size and condition progresses. The better you are, the more warm-up sets you will require. Best results will come if you split this routine and perform the first half on Monday and Thursday, the second half on Tuesday and Friday.

Johnny Fuller

## Mass-Building Routine

| Monday and Thursday | Sets | Reps |
|---|---|---|
| *Abdominals* | | |
| Roman Chair Sit-up | 2 × | 20–30 |
| *Thighs* | | |
| Squat | 6 × | 10/8/6/4/3/2 |
| *Back* | | |
| Deadlift | 4 × | 6/4/3/3 |
| T-bar Row | 6 × | 10/8/6/4/3/2 |
| *Trapezius* | | |
| Shrug | 4 × | 10/8/6/4 |
| *Biceps* | | |
| Barbell Curl | 4 × | 10/8/6/4 |
| *Calves* | | |
| Seated Calf Raise | 4 × | 15/10/10/8 |

| Tuesday and Friday | Sets | Reps |
|---|---|---|
| *Back* | | |
| Hyperextension | 2 × | 15–20 |
| *Chest* | | |
| Bench Press | 6 × | 10/8/6/4/2/2 |
| Incline Bench Press | 4 × | 10/8/6/4 |
| *Shoulders* | | |
| Press behind Neck | 4 × | 8/6/4/3 |
| Upright Row | 4 × | 8/6/4/3 |
| *Triceps* | | |
| Lying Triceps Extension | 4 × | 10/8/6/6 |

*The bench press as demonstrated by Bronston Austin, Jr.*

# BENCH PRESS ROUTINE

The bench press is the single most popular weightlifting exercise known today. The bench press develops incredible strength in three main muscle areas:

1. Shoulders (especially the anterior deltoids)
2. Arms (mainly the triceps)
3. Chest (pectorals)

The bench press is also a comfortable exercise to perform—only the arms move while the entire body is supported in the supine position. It is an exercise in which progress can come quickly and noticeably, and it is the safest of the three basic power lifts.

The bench press involves a relatively simple action, unlike the squat and deadlift, which—

even if performed in perfect style—may cause problems in the lower or upper back, or even the knee area. No injury will occur when bench pressing, as long as the bar is raised and lowered under control, and you warm up first with a lighter weight.

Strict form is essential when you start using heavy weights in the bench press. Get into the habit of holding the bar tightly when power benching. In addition to grip, it is important that you adopt a solid position on the bench. Plant both feet firmly on the ground, spaced for balance alongside the bench.

Start your bench press with as much explosive power as you can muster. The bar is immobile at the chest. It requires a strong impetus to really move it. Never bounce the bar from the chest. This could damage your sternum. Raise and lower the bar from the nipple area for maximum strength. Do not turn your head, raise your buttocks, arch your back excessively, or alter the position of your feet. Strive to keep the bar horizontal as you raise it upwards.

Beginners who want to specialize in building strength should train with the following routine three days a week with at least one rest day between workouts. To prevent one-

*Bertil Fox*

sided development, it is also advised that you do one basic exercise for the other major body parts, and that each is performed for three sets of 6–8 reps.

## Beginner's Bench Press Routine

|  | *Sets* | | *Reps* |
|---|---|---|---|
| **Monday** | | | |
| Bench Press | 1 | × | 15 |
|  | 1 | × | 10 |
|  | 2 | × | 5 |
|  | 3 | × | 2 |
|  | 1 | × | 6 |
| **Wednesday** | | | |
| Bench Press | 1 | × | 15 |
|  | 1 | × | 10 |
|  | 2 | × | 5 |
|  | 3 | × | 2 |
|  | 1 | × | 6 |
| **Friday** | | | |
| Bench Press | 1 | × | 15 |
|  | 1 | × | 6 |
|  | 1 | × | 4 |
|  | 2 | × | 2 |
|  | 1 | × | 1 (limit lift) |
|  | 1 | × | 6 |

The following is a basic bench press routine for the intermediate or advanced bodybuilder. Use this routine twice a week only and allow at least two days off from bench pressing after each workout. As with the previous schedule, you should round out the routine with basic exercises for the other body parts, performing just three sets to keep them in proportion. Attempt a new maximum "limit" lift about every three weeks.

## Advanced Bench Press Routine

|  | *Sets* | | *Reps* |
|---|---|---|---|
| Bench Press | 1 | × | 15 |
|  | 1 | × | 10 |
|  | 1 | × | 6 |
|  | 1 | × | 3 |
|  | 2 | × | 2 |
|  | 2 | × | 1 |
|  | 1 | × | 10 |

# HEAVY-AND-LIGHT ROUTINE

Bodybuilding greats Reg Park and Bill Pearl both used a system of heavy-and-light training to build their title-winning physiques. In the same workout they trained the same muscle groups using both high poundage with low reps, and low poundage and high reps.

Today modern experts agree that there is evidence to show that their reasoning was sound. High reps and low reps give different results, and each can contribute size to a body part that the other cannot.

Do not confuse *light* repetitions with *fast* repetitions. Mike Mentzer said:

> When the speed of a repetition exceeds a certain rate, momentum comes into play and thereby reduces muscular contraction. What's happening, of course, is that the weight is being thrown, not lifted. Fast repetitions are unproductive and dangerous.

For both light and heavy reps, initiate a deliberate lifting action that enables the muscles to feel the strain. It's often a good idea to pause momentarily at the top of the contracted position, then lower the weight consciously under full control.

*Roger Daggitt uses an incredible amount of weight for incline dumbbell flyes.*

*Mr. International Scott Wilson*

There are two methods involved in this technique:

1. You can perform several sets of an exercise with heavy weights (and low reps), and then perform some light sets (with high reps) using the *same* exercise.

2. You can perform a basic (multi-joint) exercise using heavy weights, and then, after several heavy sets, you can change to an isolation (lighter exercise) and use high reps for three or four sets.

## Heavy-and-Light Routine (same exercises)

|  | Sets | Reps |
|---|---|---|
| *Shoulders* | | |
| Press behind Neck | 4 × | 5 |
| | 3 × | 12 |
| *Thighs* | | |
| Squat | 4 × | 4 |
| | 3 × | 15 |

|  | Sets | Reps |
|---|---|---|
| *Chest* | | |
| Bench Press | 5 × | 5 |
| | 4 × | 12 |
| *Back* | | |
| T-bar Row | 4 × | 4 |
| | 4 × | 15 |
| *Biceps* | | |
| Barbell Curl | 4 × | 5 |
| | 3 × | 15 |
| *Triceps* | | |
| Close-grip Bench Press | 4 × | 5 |
| | 3 × | 12 |
| *Calves* | | |
| Calf Raise | 4 × | 8 |
| | 3 × | 25 |
| *Abdominals* | | |
| Roman Chair Sit-up | 3 × | 10 |
| | 3 × | 50 |

## Heavy-and-Light Routine (different exercises)

|  | Sets | Reps |
|---|---|---|
| *Shoulders* | | |
| Press behind Neck | 4 × | 5 |
| Incline Lateral Raise (with face towards bench) | 3 × | 12 |
| *Thighs* | | |
| Squat | 4 × | 4 |
| Hack Slide | 4 × | 12 |
| *Chest* | | |
| Bench Press | 5 × | 4 |
| Incline Flye | 4 × | 15 |
| *Back* | | |
| T-bar Row | 5 × | 5 |
| Lat-machine Pulldown (wide grip) | 4 × | 15 |
| *Biceps* | | |
| Barbell Curl | 4 × | 5 |
| High Bench Flat Curl | 4 × | 15 |
| *Triceps* | | |
| Close-grip Bench Press | 4 × | 4 |
| Lat-machine Pressdown | 4 × | 12 |
| *Abdominals* | | |
| Roman Chair Sit-up | 4 × | 10 |
| Crunch | 3 × | 25 |
| *Calves* | | |
| Seated Calf Raise | 4 × | 10 |
| Calf Raise | 4 × | 25 |

*Rachel McLish reps out with a cable lateral raise.*

# HOLISTIC ROUTINE

Bodybuilding entrepreneur Joe Weider said:

Bodybuilding today has become holistic. This means that an individual's training must fit in with the lifestyle, emotions, and mentality. Fitness and health must all be part of a multi-faceted system in which each part must be considered in its relationship with the others. The components of our physical, mental, and spiritual natures do not operate independently of each other.

To be a complete bodybuilder, you should not merely dwell on heavy weight training. You have to consider overall fitness, diet, rest, recuperation, and emotional stability. The holistic bodybuilder does not abuse his or her physique with poor health habits and nutritionally inferior food. If 100 percent honesty is not part of your daily routine, then make the change now.

Years ago, the holistic bodybuilder was called a *physical culturist*. As well as weight training for a proportionate physique, the physical culturist was also adept at a variety of sports and activities. The following is a good, all-around routine that should be coupled with a well-balanced diet to maximize results. Perform it, two or three times a week, with a two- to three-mile run (five to ten miles on a bicycle) on off days.

## Holistic Routine

|  | Sets | Reps |
|---|---|---|
| Rope Jumping | 2 × | 4 min. |
| *Shoulders, Back, Thighs* | | |
| Squat Clean and Jerk | 1 × | 6 |
| *Thighs* | | |
| Free-standing Squat (no weight) | 1 × | 100 |
| *Chest* | | |
| Dumbbell Bench Press | 5 × | 8 |
| Parallel Bar Dip (wide grip) | 4 × | 12 |

| Back | Sets Reps | |
|---|---|---|
| Wide-grip Chin to Chest | 4 × 10 | |
| Hyperextension | 3 × 25 | |
| *Triceps* | | |
| Lying Triceps Stretch | 3 × 12 | |
| *Trapezius* | | |
| Shrug | 5 × 3 | |
| *Biceps* | | |
| Barbell Curl | 3 × 12 | |
| *Abdominals* | | |
| Hanging Leg Raise | 3 × 20 | |

# FOUR-SIDES-TO-A-MUSCLE ROUTINE

Trainer Vince Gironda believes that each muscle has four sides for developing. Prior to the Iron Guru's four-sides-to-a-muscle moniker, the technique was known as multi-angular training. In fact, the great Mohamed Makkawy has adopted some of this technique for his V.A.T. (Variable Angle Training) programs, which are becoming extremely popular. It's a great method.

Multi-angular training signifies the working of a muscle from different angles, in order to work all possible muscle fibres. This can be accomplished more effectively these days than ever before in the history of the sport. Today there are hundreds of companies producing a wide variety of apparatus—multi-angular benches, cables and pulley apparatus, single exercise units, multi-purpose machines—almost all of which help us to hit particular muscles from different angles.

There is, of course, a slight drawback to the system. In order to work every muscle from all four sides, you must work each muscle with at least four different exercises. This makes for a pretty long workout. For that reason, you should split the workout in two (or even three)

parts. Then you will be able to do justice to the allocated exercises. However, there is no reason why you must apply multi-angular training to every muscle area. You may only wish to use it for a particular body part.

## Four-Sides-to-a-Muscle Routine

| Shoulders | Sets Reps | |
|---|---|---|
| Press behind Neck | 4 × 8 | |
| Incline Dumbbell Lateral (face towards bench) | 4 × 12 | |

*(continued on next page)*

*Mohamed Makkawy shows remarkable muscle striations.*

*Broomstick twists are excellent for trimming Serge Nubret's waistline.*

| | Sets | Reps |
|---|---|---|
| Standing Lateral Raise | 4 × | 10 |
| Alternate Dumbbell Forward Raise | 4 × | 10 |
| *Thighs* | | |
| Back Squat | 4 × | 6–8 |
| Thigh Curl | 4 × | 12 |
| Hack Slide | 4 × | 10 |
| Lunge | 4 × | 15 |
| *Chest* | | |
| Flat Bench Press | 6 × | 6–8 |
| Incline Bench Press | 4 × | 10 |
| Wide-grip Parallel Bar Dip | 4 × | 8 |
| Decline Bench Flyes | 4 × | 10 |
| *Back* | | |
| T-bar Row | 4 × | 8 |
| Wide-grip Chins behind Neck | 4 × | 10 |
| Pulldown (palms parallel) | 4 × | 12 |
| Seated Low Pulley Row | 4 × | 12 |
| *Biceps* | | |
| Barbell Curl | 4 × | 6–8 |
| Preacher Bench Curl (90 degrees) | 4 × | 8 |
| Preacher Bench Curl (35 degrees) | 4 × | 10 |
| Incline Dumbbell Curl | 4 × | 8 |
| *Triceps* | | |
| Close-grip Bench Press | 4 × | 6–8 |
| Cradle Bench Triceps Pulley (face down) | 4 × | 12 |
| Lat Machine Pressdowns | 4 × | 12 |
| Dumbbell Triceps Bent-over Kickback | 4 × | 10 |
| *Calves* | | |
| Donkey Calf Raise (toes straight forward) | 3 × | 25 |
| Toe Raise (toes pointing inwards on leg-press machine) | 3 × | 20 |
| Standing Calf Machine (toes pointing outwards) | 3 × | 20 |
| Seated Calf Raise | 2 × | 15–20 |
| *Midsection* | | |
| Broomstick Twist | 2 × | 200 |
| Hyperextension | 3 × | 12–20 |
| Hanging Knee Raise | 3 × | 15–20 |
| Crunch | 3 × | 15 |

*Gladys Portugues*

# HARD GAINER'S ROUTINE

Hard gainers are those people who have a difficult time putting on weight and muscle size. In the past it was believed that all hard gainers were small-boned—indicated when an individual's wrist measured less than seven inches. Today it is accepted that muscle development potential is not predetermined by the fact that your bone size is considered small, medium, or large. It depends on the number of muscle cells that you possess.

It just so happens that small-boned people often have a smaller allocation of muscle cells. Their muscles are usually shorter than the average length. Big-boned people frequently have longer muscles. Since no one has as yet reached his or her fullest potential, all the blame cannot be placed on unfavorable genetics.

In contrast to genetic superiors such as Mike Mentzer, Boyer Coe, Sergio Oliva, Lee Haney, Casey Viator, and Scott Wilson, the hard gainer has to pay attention to all aspects of training. A genetic superior can eat junk food—a hard gainer cannot. A genetic superior can train haphazardly and irregularly—a hard gainer cannot.

If you have reason to believe that you are a hard gainer, then you will have to buckle down to better training, regular workouts, superior nutrition, and optimal recuperation. In other words, you cannot afford to stray from the straight and narrow path of success!

## Hard Gainer's Routine

| | Sets | Reps |
|---|---|---|
| *Chest* | | |
| Medium-grip Bench Press (elbows back) | 5 | × 6 |
| Bent-arm Flye | 3 | × 12 |
| *Legs* | | |
| Back Squat (feet on block) | 4 | × 8 |
| Leg Press | 3 | × 12 |

*(continued on next page)*

| Shoulders | Sets | Reps |
|---|---|---|
| Press behind Neck (from racks) | 4 | × 6 |
| Lateral Raise (45 degrees, facing incline bench) | 3 | × 10 |
| *Back* | | |
| Medium-grip Chin (elbows back) | 4 | × 10 |
| T-bar Row | 3 | × 10 |
| *Biceps* | | |
| Standing Dumbbell Curl | 4 | × 8 |
| Incline Dumbbell Curl (35 degrees) | 3 | × 10 |
| *Triceps* | | |
| Lying Triceps Stretch | 4 | × 8 |
| Close-grip Bench Press | 3 | × 10 |
| *Abdominals* | | |
| Crunch | 2 | × 15 |

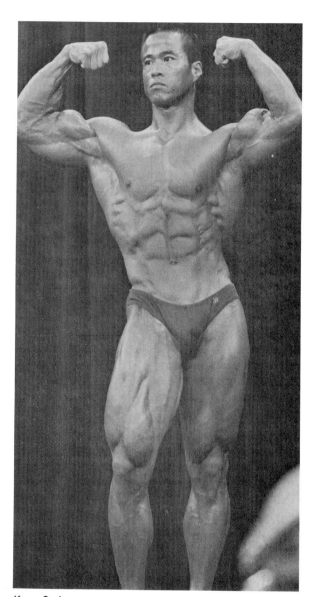

Kozo Sudo

Dinah Anderson

# CHILDREN'S ROUTINE

Children who are interested in weight training should be given short routines three times a week with each workout day followed by a day of rest. Everyday training is also acceptable if the enthusiasm level is genuinely high. The most important part of training children is to supervise each set, making sure that perfect exercise style is maintained.

Whereas a child can be encouraged to train regularly using a formal routine, other physical activities should not be ignored. Encourage youngsters to be involved in all forms of sports and games, otherwise a one-sided aspect to physical training will develop. Most champion bodybuilders were very active as children in sports such as hockey, swimming, football, gymnastics, and dance before devoting all their time to training. A youth growing up only on weight training will not learn the important motor skills of balance and coordination that result from practicing different sports.

The American Academy of Pediatrics (AAP) is opposed to weight training by preadolescents and warns that heavy lifts should not be attempted until young people are sixteen or seventeen years old.

According to Dr. Michael Yessis, publisher of the *Soviet Sports Review*:

> Most medical professionals have little, if any, comprehension of weight training. They fear that children who lift weights too soon will develop high-blood pressure, epiphyseal damage, which interferes with normal growth, and injuries of the back, shoulders, and legs. . . . In the Soviet Union no such discrepancy of confusion as to when youngsters should begin lifting exists. The Soviets generally accept that prepubescent children 11–13 years old can and do lift weights.

## Children's Routine

| | Sets | Reps |
|---|---|---|
| Standing Barbell Press (Shoulders) | 1 | × 12 |
| Squat (Legs) | 1 | × 10 |
| Bench Press (Chest) | 2 | × 8 |
| Bent-over Row (Back) | 1 | × 10 |
| Bent-knee Sit-up (Abdominals) | 1 | × 12 |
| Barbell Curl (Biceps) | 1 | × 8 |
| Triceps Standing Stretch (Triceps) | 1 | × 10 |

*Russian champion Olev Annus*

# OVER-FORTY ROUTINE

Certainly, people who *start* weight training at forty, should take it easy. First get a medical checkup, then follow the beginner's routine (see page 92). This is very important if you haven't indulged in formal exercise for a few years, or if you are a heavy smoker. Men will find that the testosterone level diminishes around the forties, and women and men both notice a decided slowing down of the metabolism. In order to stay trim, the answer, of course, is to eat fewer overall calories.

Vince Gironda doesn't see middle age as a drawback to physical conditioning. In fact, he won the title for his height class at the NABBA Mr. Universe at the age of forty-five, back in the early 1960s. "One thing I would caution older trainers," says the Iron Guru, "they should concentrate on quality nutrition. You may be able to get by on burgers and fries in your younger years, but the older bodybuilder must go for the better foods and forget the junk."

You can add sets as you get accustomed to your training, but never make your routine too long and arduous. Long routines will bore you, and then it will only become a matter of time before you lose interest in your workout. Also be sure to warm up well before each exercise. One set of 20–25 reps for each new exercise is recommended. Two or three warm-up sets are necessary for the upper legs.

*Joe Gold, the owner of the World Gym, can bench press a hefty weight—and he's over sixty years old!*

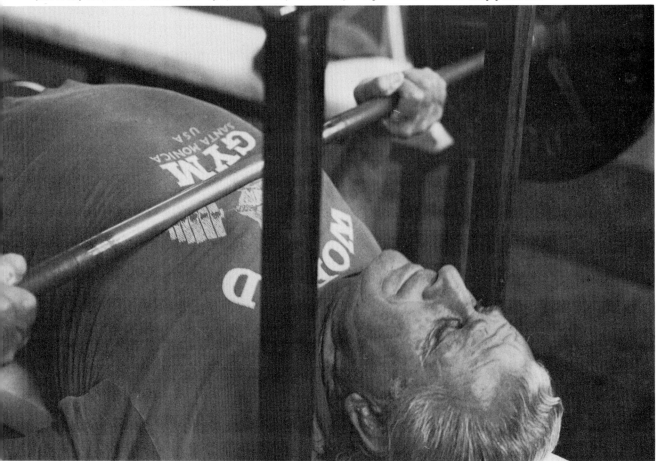

## Over-Forty Routine

| | Sets | Reps |
|---|---|---|
| Rope Jumping | 3 × | 1½ min. |
| *Shoulders* | | |
| Seated Dumbbell Press | 3 × | 12 |
| *Chest* | | |
| Bench Press | 5 × | 10 |
| *Thighs* | | |
| Squat | 3 × | 15 |
| Thigh Extension | 3 × | 12 |
| *Calves* | | |
| Standing Calf Raise | 3 × | 20 |
| *Back* | | |
| Wide-grip Lat-machine Pulldown | 2 × | 10 |
| *Triceps* | | |
| Close-grip Lat-machine Pulldown | 2 × | 10 |
| Close-grip Parallel Bar Dip | 2 × | 10 |
| *Biceps* | | |
| Incline Dumbbell Curl | 3 × | 10 |
| *Abdominals* | | |
| Crunch | 3 × | 15–20 |

# OVER-SIXTY ROUTINE

More and more people of advanced years are interested in bodybuilding methods. The beauty of weight training is that you can tailor the resistance to your individual physical condition. Those who are reaching their sixties or over can use bodybuilding methods to keep their muscles well developed and elastic. Many sixty-plus individuals have made remarkable progress from pumping iron, especially when their efforts have been tied in with a sound diet.

If you are underweight, then try eating more natural carbohydrates, whole grains, fruits, vegetables, and more fish. Eggs, red meats, and cheese are good foods but high in animal fat, which could increase cholesterol levels.

Those who desire to lose weight should go about it gradually. Do not try to shed pounds of fat by exercise alone. It simply will not happen. In fact, a strict diet by itself is not good for the body. Dieting without exercise leaves you without energy or muscle tone. Depression can set in because you are not stimulating the metabolism. Actually, a severe diet can cause the body to downcycle the metabolism, and you may end up gaining weight inspite of drastically reducing caloric intake.

The answer is to reduce your calories moderately and exercise regularly. Remember that key word—*moderation*. See your doctor before you start any health and fitness programs, and take a simple stress test. Get into the habit of walking again. This is still one of the most beneficial exercises. The next time you go to work or to a shopping plaza, arrive fifteen minutes early and park the car half a mile away from your destination. Walk there and back, and adopt a regular walking routine. Joe Gold, the originator of Gold's Gym and current owner of the World Gym, now in his sixties, walks for miles on the Santa Monica beach every day.

When you do the following weight-training program, start with very light weights and do all the exercises in perfect exercise style.

## Over-Sixty Routine

| | Sets | Reps |
|---|---|---|
| Running in Place (2–3 minutes) | | |
| *Chest* | | |
| Bench Press | 2 × | 15–20 |
| *Shoulders* | | |
| Standing Dumbbell Press | 2 × | 12 |
| *Thighs* | | |
| Leg Press | 2 × | 12 |
| Thigh Extension | 2 × | 20 |
| *Triceps* | | |
| Close-grip Lat-machine Pulldown | 2 × | 15 |
| Lying Triceps Stretch | 2 × | 10 |
| *Biceps* | | |
| Seated Dumbbell Curl | 2 × | 10 |
| *Abdominals* | | |
| Seated Knee Raise | 3 × | 20 |
| High-knee Walking in Place (2–3 minutes) | | |

# Part VI

# PROGRAMS FOR SPECIALIZATION

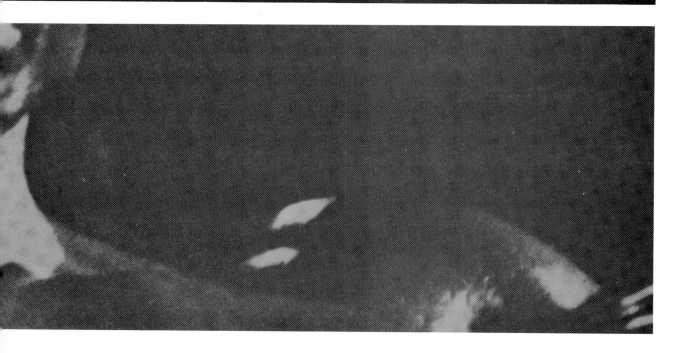

*Sergio Oliva*

The term *specialization* isn't used much today, but the method is used extensively. The purpose is to devote a major portion of your workout to the development of one particular body part. In most cases, this is a body part that needs additional development to match the other muscles of the physique. Very few bodybuilders have equal growth in all areas even when each body part is trained with an identical number of sets and reps.

When doing a specialization routine you can use a variety of high-intensity methods (though not in the same workout) such as pre-exhaust, supersets, trisets, compound sets, and progressions up and down the rack (as described in Part IV). It is advised, for the most part, to use strict exercise form on the area of specialization. This conserves energy and helps you to hit the muscle solidly. Use full-range movements to attain maximum shape and muscle isolation. Always start your training by working the specialized area first. Don't specialize on any one area for more than eight weeks. Simply perform a more balanced routine for a period, after which you can return to another specialization program on the same area or another body part.

The important point to remember about this method is that you also work the rest of the body. Specialization never means training one body part to the exclusion of all others. The plan is to push hard at one lagging area with lots of sets, reps, and intensity, in addition to developing the rest of the body with basic maintenance sets.

*Mohamed Makkawy's upper arm is truly astounding.*

Your specialization routine should include from 15–25 sets (depending on your physical condition and tolerance to strenuous weight training). At least four different exercises should be employed; twenty sets of one exercise is not as advantageous as five sets of four exercises. The variety hits the muscle from different angles and better results will become evident.

It is recommended that you specialize on only one body part at a time. You cannot really do justice to more than one area if you are trying to make outstanding gains.

As a general rule, a large body part (thighs, back, chest) needs two workouts a week to develop noticeably. Three workouts a week are necessary for other body parts (arms, shoulders) and five- or six-day-per-week workouts are required to improve calves or forearms.

# UPPER-ARM SPECIALIZATION

Well-developed, proportionate arms are important goals for most bodybuilders. They must be relatively fat free, otherwise they will have zero impact when you flex them! Fat hides the three heads of the triceps and combines them into a single unimpressive bulge. Fat also de-emphasizes the shape of the biceps.

Bulked-out bodybuilders, wrestlers, or powerlifters could display a big and formidable arm but never a *great* arm, which requires careful shaping. If building bulk is your passion, then however hard you train you will never be able to sculpt majestic arms equal to those found on men such as Robby Robinson, Al Beckles, Bill Grant, and Mohamed Makkawy.

In specializing on the upper arms, choose four biceps exercises and four triceps exercises. Select movements that hit different

*Lance Dreher*

parts of each area. At least one movement should be a basic exercise such as the regular barbell curl for the biceps and the close-grip bench press for the triceps. Employ low reps with heavy weight, a moderate number with medium weight, and high reps with lighter weight. In this way, you cover all bases and have the greatest chance for success. The following is a straight-set routine for upper-arm specialization, including the exercises to maintain the rest of the body.

## Upper-Arm Specialization Routine

| | Sets Reps |
|---|---|
| Barbell Curl (Upper and Middle Biceps) | 4 × 6 |
| Incline Dumbbell Curl (Middle Biceps) | 4 × 8 |
| 90-degree Preacher Bench Curl (Peak) | 4 × 8 |
| 35-degree Preacher Bench Curl (Lower Biceps) | 4 × 10 |
| | |
| Close-grip Bench Press (Triceps Belly) | 4 × 6 |
| Parallel Bar Dip (Middle Triceps) | 4 × 8 |
| Lying Triceps Stretch (Upper Triceps) | 4 × 8 |
| Single-arm Dumbbell Triceps Curl (Lower Triceps) | 4 × 12 |
| | |
| Squat (Thighs) | 3 × 10 |
| Press behind Neck (Shoulders) | 3 × 8 |
| T-bar Row (Upper Back) | 3 × 8 |
| Bench Press (Chest) | 3 × 8 |
| Calf Raise (Lower Legs) | 3 × 15 |
| Crunch (Abdominals) | 3 × 15 |

If you do not wish to work the arms with straight sets, you could use the pre-exhaust method. For example, do straight sets with the barbell curl and then alternate five sets of 90-degree preacher bench curls (isolation movement) with narrow-undergrip chins (combination movement).

For triceps, first perform four straight sets of close-grip bench presses followed by five sets of pressdowns on the lat machine (isolation movement) alternating with parallel bar dips (combination movement.) Always remember that the pre-exhaust technique requires that the isolation movement be followed immediately by the combination movement.

## Pre-Exhaust Upper-Arm Routine

| | | Sets Reps |
|---|---|---|
| Barbell Curl (Upper and Middle Biceps) | | 4 × 6–8 |
| 90-degree Preacher Bench Curl (Peak) | alternate | 5 × 10 |
| Undergrip Chin (Biceps Belly) | | 5 × 8–12 |
| Close-grip Bench Press (Triceps Belly) | | 4 × 6–8 |
| Lat-machine Pressdown (Upper Triceps) | alternate | 5 × 10 |
| Parallel Bar Dip (Middle Triceps) | | 5 × 10 |

**Tips**   For the outer head of the biceps (which can be seen from the back in the double biceps pose), try seated concentration curls with hypersupination, turning the hand up and as far around as possible as the curl is completed. For the brachialis muscle, do thumbs-up hammer curls with dumbbells. Preacher curls, with dumbbells or barbells, work the biceps in the lower regions when the bench angle is shallow (almost flat) and the middle and upper regions (peak) when it is fixed at a steeper angle, all the way to 90 degrees.

The outer head of the triceps is activated in all triceps exercises in which the elbows are positioned considerably wider than the hands (for example, keeping the elbows out during the pulley pressdown exercise). The lower triceps area (near the elbow) is activated in peak-contraction movements such as bent-over triceps kickbacks. Upper triceps (near the shoulder) are brought into action in the lying (supine) triceps stretch.

# BACK SPECIALIZATION

Although the back is comprised of numerous muscles, for the sake of simplification there are four main aspects in back training:

1. *Width* (latissimus muscles)
2. *Density* (muscle mass and deep crevices between the muscles)
3. *Lower back* (solidly developed erectus spinae and surrounding area)
4. *Trapezius* (muscles at the base of the neck and upper back).

Most back exercises utilize muscles of other areas, but specific problems should nevertheless be tackled with exercise techniques and combinations tailored to rectify weaknesses in particular areas.

If you have good muscle density in the back, but lack sufficient V-shape and latissimus width, then you must go beyond a simple back-building routine. You must work to spread out the lats and underlying bones of the scapula (the shoulder blades). The same goes for the person who has little muscle density, poor traps or lower back. The problem must be solved with a specifically adapted schedule of exercises.

## Back-Specialization Routine

|  | Sets | Reps |
|---|---|---|
| Chin behind Neck (Lat Width) | 4 × | 10–15 |
| T-bar Row (Back Density) | 4 × | 6 |
| Parallel-grip Pulldown (Overall Back) | 4 × | 12 |
| Seated Pulley Cable Row (Overall Back) | 4 × | 12 |
| Prone Hyperextension (Lower Back) | 4 × | 15 |
| | | |
| Bench Press (Chest) | 3 × | 10 |
| Press behind Neck (Shoulders) | 3 × | 8 |
| Squat (Thighs) | 3 × | 10 |

Look at the great definition in Samir Bannout's lower back.

(continued on next page)

| | Sets | Reps |
|---|---|---|
| Calf Raise (Lower Legs) | 3 | × 15 |
| Barbell Curl (Biceps) | 3 | × 8 |
| Triceps Stretch (Triceps) | 3 | × 10 |
| Crunch (Abdominals) | 3 | × 15 |

## V-Shape Back Routine

| | Sets | Reps |
|---|---|---|
| Wide-grip Chin behind Neck | 5 | × 10 |
| Wide-grip Pulldown behind Neck | 5 | × 10 |
| Single-arm Dumbbell Row | 5 | × 8 |
| Bent-arm Pullover | 5 | × 6–10 |

**Tips**    Back width comes from stretching the shoulder blades *out* from the body. This is easier for eighteen-year-olds to do than it is for thirty-year-olds, but even so, older people have managed to mobilize the scapula to create the V-shape effect. Endeavor to stretch out the shoulder blades at various times during the day by pulling on stationary objects.

Do not hang weights from your waist when chinning for back width. Using additional weight will only serve to recruit the arms in helping the chinning action. At the conclusion

*Mr. Olympia Samir Bannout*

of a set of chins or pulldowns, hang on to the bar for an additional ten seconds. Feel the shoulder blades stretch even more. When performing wide-grip exercises there is a tendency to do half reps, but better development comes from full reps, pulling the bar up to the back of the neck and then extending the arms completely. Always keep the elbows spread far apart. Remember, wide-grip chins and pulldowns are superior to close-grip movements when it comes to stretching the lats.

## Back Routine for Mass and Thickness

| | Sets | Reps |
|---|---|---|
| T-bar Row | 5 × | 6 |
| Parallel-grip Pulldown | 5 × | 10 |
| Seated Pulley Cable Row | 5 × | 12 |
| Medium-grip Chin to Chest | 5 × | 10 |

**Tips**    T-bar rowing is safer than bent-over rowing since one end of the resistance is fixed. This enables the exerciser to set his or her position carefully so that minimum stress is placed on the lower back. When doing the cable rows squeeze the shoulder blades together as you complete the rep and stretch forward as the arms straighten.

## Lower-Back Routine

| | Sets | Reps |
|---|---|---|
| Power Clean | 4 × | 6 |
| Prone Hyperextension | 4 × | 12 |
| Stiff-legged Deadlift | 4 × | 12 |
| Good-morning Exercise | 3 × | 10 |

**Tips**    The best lower back in bodybuilding today belongs to Mr. Olympia Samir Bannout. His early training as an Olympic weightlifter included cleans and deadlifts, and he credits much of his success to this. By far, the safest lower-back exercise is the prone hyperextension because there is no downward pressure on the vertebrae, as is the case when performing most lower-back movements. *Caution: Do not begin a lower-back specialization program using heavy weights.* Human beings are highly susceptible to lower-back injuries. Always use relatively light weights at first.

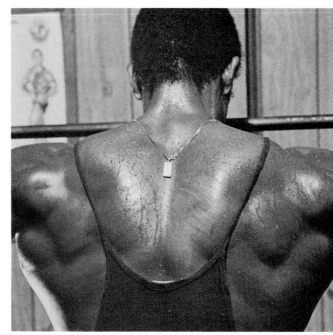

*The ultrathick back of Serge Nubret*

## Trapezius Routine

| | Sets | Reps |
|---|---|---|
| Deadlift | 4 × | 6 |
| Shoulder Shrug | 5 × | 10 |
| Close-grip Upright Row | 5 × | 12 |
| Medium-grip Cable Pulldown | 5 × | 12 |

**Tips**    Well-developed traps do not detract from your overall back width, unless you have a very short neck, in which case you shouldn't do any direct trapezius work. The biggest traps in bodybuilding today belong to Lou Ferrigno and Serge Nubret.

You can do your shoulder shrugs on a Universal machine, on a standing calf machine, or by using barbells and dumbbells. Each produces a slightly different effect; if you start feeling bored during your workout, substitute some different exercises in your routine.

The traps begin at the base of the neck, continuing down the middle of the back. Activate this area by tensing the muscles when you bring the bar down during wide-grip cable pulldowns behind the neck. Take the bar as far down the back as possible. The traps will pop out quickly if, in addition to the above specialization schedule, you practice the "most muscular" pose.

# SHOULDER SPECIALIZATION

Wide shoulders are always a plus in bodybuilding. Even people with narrow or medium shoulder width can look broad if they build their shoulders up sufficiently, especially the lateral (side) head. Of course, individuals with the widest shoulders have natural width *and* maximum muscle mass.

Since the shoulders are composed of three heads or sections of muscle (the deltoids), it is imperative that any training program for shoulder development incorporates exercises for each area—front, back, and sides.

Can a person increase the width of the shoulder clavicles, and thus shoulder width? The answer is that all-around weight training

*Mohamed Makkawy and Lee Haney*

will give a small amount of added width and thickness to the bone, but this is usually too small to be noticed.

The lateral deltoid increases your V-shape taper when seen from the front, but do not make the mistake of neglecting the other heads of the deltoid muscle. The rear head is very important because it adds visual detail in all back poses, especially when the arms are raised above the head. Equally important is the side view; without a well-built rear deltoid, you will look round shouldered from the side, and you could even lose points in a contest for appearing to have poor posture.

Even though the front deltoids get plenty of work during bench presses, they should nevertheless be worked with isolation exercises such as the dumbbell or pulley front raise. When sunlight, or stage lighting at a contest, hits the front deltoids (showing up their different plane from the upper chest) it gives the illusion of increased width, even though the front delts actually add nothing to shoulder width.

## Shoulder-Specialization Routine

| | | Sets | Reps |
|---|---|---|---|
| Seated Dumbbell Press | | 4 | × 6 |
| Press behind Neck | | 4 | × 8 |
| Upright Row | | 4 | × 10 |
| Lateral Raise | (shoulders) | 4 | × 12 |
| Bent-over Lateral | | 4 | × 12 |
| Alternate Dumbbell Forward Raise | | 4 | × 12 |
| Squat (Thighs) | | 3 | × 10 |
| Bench Press (Chest) | | 3 | × 8 |
| T-bar Row (Back) | | 3 | × 8 |
| Barbell Curl (Biceps) | | 3 | × 8 |
| Triceps Curl (Triceps) | | 3 | × 10 |
| Crunch (Abdominals) | | 3 | × 15 |

If you want to increase intensity in your shoulder-specialization program, you could use giant sets, descending sets, or up-and-down-the-rack sets. The pre-exhaust method is ideally suited for maxing out the lateral deltoids.

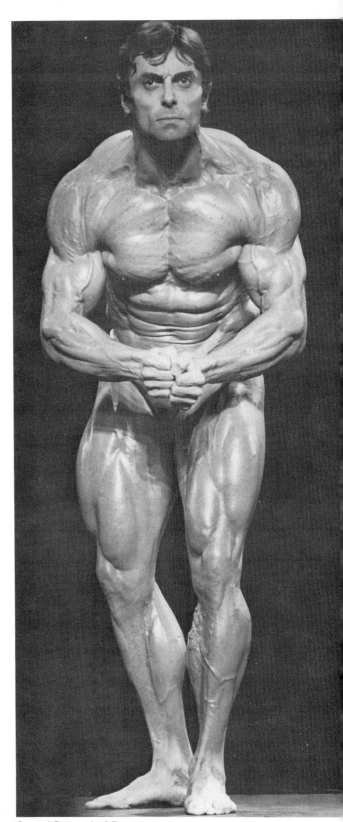

Gerard Buinoud of France

## Pre-Exhaust Shoulder Routine

|  | Sets | Reps |
|---|---|---|
| Dumbbell Lateral Raise (Isolation) } alternate | 4 | × 10 |
| Press behind Neck (Combination) | 4 | × 8 |
| Side Pulley Lateral (Isolation) } alternate | 4 | × 12 |
| Upright Row (Combination) | 4 | × 10 |

**Tips**  Always perform the combination movements immediately after the isolation exercises without any rest period in between.

The above pre-exhaust shoulder routine can be intensified by adding an exercise for the front delts (alternate dumbbell forward raise) and the rear delts (bent-over lateral). As far as exercise performance goes, your arms should always be bent on every variation of the lateral raise with dumbbells or pulleys.

When pressing barbells or dumbbells keep the elbows back and out to the sides; when performing the upright row hold the bar with a wide grip (a narrow grip only works the front delts and the trapezius).

# THIGH SPECIALIZATION

Thigh training is undeniably painful. I recall Mr. Universe Jeff King telling me that he hated squats so much that he could hardly sleep the night before a leg workout. The back squat is indeed the king of all exercises. It does stimulate your metabolic rate (and accordingly effects overall growth), but too much squatting, especially in conjunction with an overabundance of calories, can cause the hips to spread.

Whether or not you should squat flat-footed or with a two- or three-inch block under your heels is a matter of individual preference. If you find that you have to lean forward in an exaggerated stance when you squat down, then a block under your heels would be helpful. It is important when squatting that the thighs do the work, not the lower back and glutes.

One cannot say that a certain exercise works a particular part of the thigh because it depends on the aforementioned leverage factors. For example, the back squat can build the entire thigh for some people. Individuals with short legs will notice development from just above the knee to the groin area. If the long-legged bodybuilder does squats, he or she will build the upper thigh only. A hack machine is necessary to develop the lower thigh, near the knee.

How far down should you squat when performing the deep-knee bend? The answer: all the way down, unless you have weak or troublesome knees. The important consideration, however, is that you do not bounce in the low position. If you bolt upright from a low squat position, injured knees will surely come your way sooner or later. Many bodybuilders and athletes squat down only until the thighs are parallel to the floor. This may at first seem harder than going all the way down, but with practice you will find it easier on the knees.

## Thigh-Specialization Routine

|  | Sets | Reps |
|---|---|---|
| Squat (Belly of Quads) | 6 | × 8 |
| Hack Squat (Lower Thigh) | 4 | × 8 |
| Leg Extension (Middle and Lower Thigh) | 4 | × 10 |
| Leg Press (Overall Quads) | 4 | × 12 |
| Leg Curl (Thigh Biceps) | 4 | × 12 |
| Pulley Leg Squeeze (Inner Sartorius) | 4 | × 12 |
| Press behind Neck (Shoulders) | 3 | × 8 |
| Bench Press (Chest) | 3 | × 8 |
| T-bar Row (Back) | 3 | × 10 |
| Calf Raise (Lower Legs) | 3 | × 15 |
| Barbell Curl (Biceps) | 3 | × 8 |
| Triceps Curl (Triceps) | 3 | × 10 |
| Crunch (Abdominals) | 3 | × 15 |

Jeff King

*Deanna Panting has admirably well-shaped legs.*

**Tips**   Always pyramid your sets (add weight after each one) of heavy leg work, if maximum results are part of your plan.

Remember to use a wide stance or point your knees outwards when doing squats, hack squats, or leg presses to work the inner thighs. Keep the feet close together and point knees inwards to activate the outer thigh. The best exercise for the lower thigh is the sissy squat. Although the movement for the regular back squat and the leg press appears to be similar, the back squat is far superior as a mass-building exercise for the thigh.

A considerable number of trainers have underdeveloped vastus internus muscles (just above the knees). The following is a specialization routine to develop the area. Bear in mind that more emphasis can be directed on the lower thigh by placing a 2½-inch block of wood under the heels when performing back or front squats.

## Lower-Thigh Specialization Routine

| | Sets | Reps |
|---|---|---|
| Smith Machine Squat (feet forward) | 4 × | 8 |
| Hack Machine Squat (heels together) | 4 × | 10 |
| Leg Extension | 4 × | 10 |
| Sissy Squat | 4 × | 12 |
| Roman Chair Squat | 4 × | 15 |

The pre-exhaust method can be used to speed up lower-thigh development. The following routine is very strenuous.

## Pre-Exhaust Lower-Thigh Routine

| | Sets | Reps |
|---|---|---|
| Thigh Extension | 4 × | 12 |
| Front Squat | 4 × | 10 |
| Roman Chair Squat | 4 × | 15 |
| Back Squat | 4 × | 8 |

**Tips**     It is best to train the thigh region only twice weekly. You may also use the continuous-tension principle when training with the pre-exhaust thigh program. This entails the use of a "non-lock" technique when doing all forms of squats. You finish the movement when you are still a few inches away from the straight-legged position, thus cutting out the brief rest achieved when the legs lock straight. Any thigh-specialization program will confront the bodybuilder with muscle pain. There's no way around it. Work hard and your thighs will take on a whole new appearance.

# CHEST SPECIALIZATION

Most bodybuilders can build impressive pectoral muscles. Even the ectomorphic (skinny) types start to show development within their first few weeks of training. In fact,

*Robby Robinson and Tony Pearson*

*Carla Dunlap*

in some cases the pectorals grow too fast for the rest of the body, and the only thing to do is to ease up on chest exercises to work on the other muscle groups.

The biggest pecs in bodybuilding belonged to 1945 Mr. America Clarence Ross, until Reg Park came along in the 1960s. Arnold Schwarzenegger and Sergio Oliva then made everyone else's pecs look puny. Today we have a host of big-chested athletes—Lee Haney, Mike Christian, Mary Roberts, Carla Dunlap— and, of course, the inimitable Bev Francis who can bench press an amazing 350 pounds.

The best single exercise for the chest is the bench press. Indeed, many highly ranked bodybuilders have built ponderous pecs just from this one exercise. Complete results, however, come from combining the bench press with the incline press or flye movements with dumbbells. Some bodybuilders regularly perform six or even eight different chest exercises, many of which are isolation movements, as opposed to multi-joint exercises such as the bench press. Remember that there never was a bodybuilder who developed an impressive chest solely from cable crossovers, pec-deck crunches, or flye motions. If you want bulk, go with the heavy movements such as supine and incline bench presses or parallel bar dips. Use the isolation exercises in conjunction with these heavy movements.

## Chest-Specialization Routine

| | *Sets* | *Reps* |
|---|---|---|
| Bench Press (Middle Pecs) | 6 | × 6 |
| Incline Dumbbell Bench Press (Upper Pecs) | 4 | × 8 |
| Parallel Bar Dip (Lower Pecs) | 4 | × 8 |
| Decline Dumbbell Bench Press (Lower Outer Pecs) | 4 | × 10 |
| Supine Flye (Middle Outer Pecs) | 4 | × 10 |
| | | |
| Squat (Thighs) | 3 | × 10 |
| Press behind Neck (Shoulders) | 3 | × 8 |
| T-bar Row (Back) | 3 | × 10 |
| Calf Raise (Lower Legs) | 3 | × 15 |
| Barbell Curl (Biceps) | 3 | × 8 |
| Triceps Curl (Triceps) | 3 | × 10 |
| Crunch (Abominals) | 3 | × 15 |

Bev Francis can bench press 350 pounds—
an amazing feat for a woman.

**Tips** Use heavy weights in the bench press to completely stimulate muscle fibres, tendons, and ligaments. Always keep the elbows pointed outwards at right angles to the body when pressing with barbells or dumbbells. Never bounce the weights on the chest and always lower them under control when working the pectorals. All flyes must be done with bent arms, stretching downwards as far as possible.

You may want to apply the pre-exhaust method to the pectorals. This intensifies the action with less overall sets required.

## Pre-Exhaust Chest Routine

|  | Sets Reps |
|---|---|
| Supine Flye ⎫ alternate | 4 × 12 |
| Bench Press ⎭ | 4 × 10 |
| Pulley Crossover (or Pec-Deck Crunch) ⎫ alternate | 3 × 12 |
| Dumbbell Bench Press (35-degree angle) ⎭ | 3 × 10 |

**Tips** Do not rest after performing a set of flyes—proceed immediately to bench presses.

Likewise, follow the crossovers immediately with the dumbbell bench press, with no rest period.

## Upper-Chest Specialization Routine

|  | Sets Reps |
|---|---|
| Incline Barbell Bench Press | 4 × 10 |
| Incline Dumbbell Bench Press | 4 × 10 |
| Incline Flye | 4 × 10 |

**Tips** Do not perform the incline barbell bench press on an overly steep angle—35 degrees is ideal. If you train on a 45–50-degree incline bench, you will exercise the front deltoids more than the upper pectorals.

Finally, be aware that the effect of bench pressing can be varied by changing the width of your grip on the bar and by lowering the bar to specific areas of the chest. For example, a narrow grip works the inner pectorals; a wide grip develops the outer sections. Lower the bar to touch the lower chest and you will train that area more intensely; bring it to the upper pecs and the effect will be chiefly felt on the higher part of the chest.

*Al Beckles*

# CALF SPECIALIZATION

Boyer Coe and Chris Dickerson both agree that calf building can be tough. They emphasize that genetics contribute a major part, but a positive attitude coupled with an incessant drive will accomplish a great deal.

How can you develop calves that are situated high on the leg? If high calves are accompanied by a sparseness of muscle fibre, then probably no amount of heavy work will change the situation dramatically. What will help the overall appearance of the legs, and diminish the unbalanced look, is the degree in which you develop the thighs. Many sets of squats will bulk up the quads too excessively. If you cut down on squats and increase the number of hack and thigh extensions, the leg line will have better proportions.

Stretching is a very important practice for complete calf development. Boyer Coe always precedes his calf training with plenty of free-stretching movements, using only his body weight for resistance.

## Calf-Specialization Routine

|  | Sets | Reps |
|---|---|---|
| Calf Stretching (15 min.) | | |
| Standing Calf Raise (Middle Calf) | 6 × | 15–20 |
| Seated Calf Raise (Soleus) | 4 × | 15 |
| Toe Raise (leg-press machine) (Inner Calf) | 4 × | 15 |
| Donkey Calf Raise (Overall Calf) | 4 × | 15–20 |
| | | |
| Bench Press (Chest) | 3 × | 10 |
| Squat (Thighs) | 3 × | 10 |
| Press behind Neck (Shoulders) | 3 × | 8 |
| T-bar Row (Back) | 3 × | 10 |
| Barbell Curl (Biceps) | 3 × | 8 |
| Triceps Extension (Triceps) | 3 × | 10 |
| Crunch (Abdominals) | 3 × | 15 |

Danny Padilla

159

**Tips** Most calf exercises should be performed with the feet pointed straight ahead; however, at times you may want to correct the symmetry of your outer and inner calf development. Doing calf raises with the toes pointed outwards puts more of the stress on the inner calf; pointing the toes inwards stresses the outer calf. Although changing toe positions does affect different parts of the calf muscle, the change in actual development is seldom dramatic enough to be noticed.

Some bodybuilders find an advantage in unlocking the knees while performing the donkey calf raise. This can lessen the painful burning sensation, releasing lactic acid buildup considerably, enabling you to continue doing more reps. Bending the knees can also activate the soleus area.

# ABDOMINAL SPECIALIZATION

When people look at an "object," said Dennis Tinerino, "they look at the middle of it first. That's why I go all out in my abdominal training when getting ready for a bodybuilding contest." Tinerino's well-defined abdominals are symmetrically even and highly developed from top to bottom.

There are men and women with outstanding abdominal development who do not have even rows of muscle. It appears to make no difference to the judges that Lee Haney, Johnny Fuller, Tony Pearson, Ray Mentzer, Chris Dickerson, and Lynn Conkwright don't quite have perfectly symmetrical abs.

What is important is that the abdominals stand out in bold relief when they are flexed—and that the surrounding body fat is minimal. Never make the mistake of thinking that waistline exercises alone will give you abdominal impressiveness. Your diet must be strictly curtailed as well.

You can forget about using sauna belts. They only serve to hold in the waist and cause water loss from increased sweating. As soon as you drink any fluids, you will immediately regain the water weight.

For men, the largest fat-storage area is the waistline. They may have to work harder than women for top abdominal results. Women tend to store fat more on the hips and upper thighs.

## Abdominal-Specialization Routine

|  | Sets | Reps |
|---|---|---|
| Crunch (Middle Abs) | 3 × | 15 |
| Hanging Leg Raise (Lower Abs) | 3 × | 15 |
| Kneeling Rope Pull (Upper Abs) | 3 × | 12 |
| Concemetric Crunch (Middle Abs) | 3 × | 15 |
| Side Bend (with one dumbbell) (Obliques) | 3 × | 20 |
| Press behind Neck (Shoulders) | 3 × | 8 |
| Squat (Thighs) | 3 × | 8 |
| Bench Press (Chest) | 3 × | 8 |
| T-bar Row (Back) | 3 × | 10 |
| Barbell Curl (Biceps) | 3 × | 8 |
| Triceps Extension (Triceps) | 3 × | 10 |
| Calf Raise (Lower Legs) | 3 × | 15 |

**Tips** The waistline area is well suited to the giant sets principle, which means to perform one set of each exercise, one after the other, until you have done all five abdominal exercises. Then start again with the first ab movement, and repeat them for a total of three cycles. Rest minimally between exercises.

Some bodybuilders have poorly developed lower abdominals in relation to the upper area (it never seems to be the other way around). The following specialization program is designed to develop the lower abdominals.

## Lower-Abdominal Specialization Routine

|  | Sets | Reps |
|---|---|---|
| Hanging Leg Raise (Lower Abs) | 4 × | 12 |
| Seated Knee Raise (Lower and Middle Abs) | 4 × | 15 |
| Inverted Sit-up (with gravity boots) (Lower Abs) | 4 × | 12 |

*Ed Kawak has almost perfectly symmetrical abdominal muscles.*

# Part VII

# ROUTINES OF THE CHAMPIONS

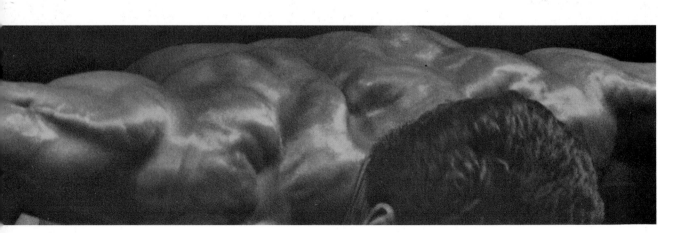

*Bob Paris*

**P**eople are fascinated by the way champion bodybuilders train. They are curious to know which exercises helped to create such impressive muscles. There are two points to remember when checking out a champion's routine:

1. Like anyone else, champions constantly change their exercises. They adopt a specific routine to achieve certain results. Few stay with the same routine all the time.

2. What suits one person may not suit another. If you were short, stocky, and big boned, it wouldn't make sense to base your routine on Steve Reeves's training. If you are determined to try someone else's routine, then choose someone who is similar to your own body structure.

For whatever reason you want to know, here are the routines of some of the biggest names in the bodybuilding world.

# SAMIR BANNOUT

Mr. Olympia Samir Bannout—the man with perfect shape and the "master of symmetry"—was born in Beirut, Lebanon. In his own words, he was "an incredible pencil neck" before taking up bodybuilding. However, through dedication, he added over 100 pounds of muscle to his frame and won the Mr. World, Mr. Universe, and Mr. Olympia titles. Samir likes to perform a combination of heavy and light exercises when training each muscle group.

*Samir Bannout*

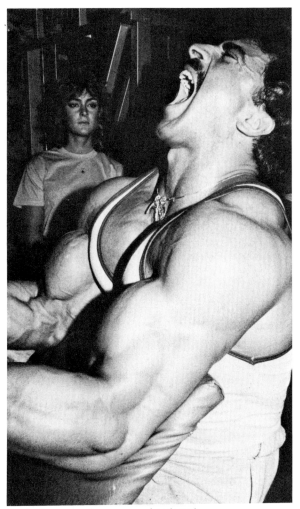

*Samir does a curl on a preacher bench.*

## Routine

|  | Sets | Reps |
|---|---|---|
| **Monday, Wednesday, Friday** A.M. | | |
| *Shoulders* | | |
| Press behind Neck | 5 × | 8–12 |
| Lateral Raise | 4 × | 10–12 |
| Bent-over Rear Deltoid Flye ⎱ superset | 5 × | 10–12 |
| Upright Row ⎰ | | |
| *Arms* | | |
| Seated Curl ⎱ superset | | |
| Triceps Pushdown ⎰ | 4 × | 8 |
| Seated Alternate Dumbbell Curl ⎱ superset | | |
| French Press ⎰ | 4 × | 8–10 |
| Concentration Curl ⎱ superset | | |
| Parallel Bar Dip ⎰ | 4 × | 8–10 |

Samir Bannout

**Monday, Wednesday, Friday** P.M.

*Calves*

| | Sets | Reps |
|---|---|---|
| Standing Calf Raise | 4 × | 10–15 |
| Seated Calf Raise | 4 × | 10–15 |
| Calf Raise (on leg-press machine) | 4 × | 10–15 |

*Abdominals*

| | Sets | Reps |
|---|---|---|
| Knee-up | 4 × | 25 |
| Sit-up | 4 × | 25 |
| Crunch | 4 × | 25 |

**Tuesday, Thursday, Saturday** A.M.

*Chest*

| | Sets | Reps |
|---|---|---|
| Bench Press | 4 × | 8 |
| Incline Press | 4 × | 6–8 |
| Bench Flye | 4 × | 8 |
| Dips (with weight) | 4 × | 8 |

*Back*

| | Sets | Reps |
|---|---|---|
| Lat Pulldown | 4 × | 10–12 |
| Bent-over Row | 4 × | 10–12 |
| Cable Pulley | 4 × | 10–12 |
| Chin | 4 × | 10–12 |

**Tuesday, Thursday, Saturday** P.M.

*Legs*

| | Sets | Reps |
|---|---|---|
| Squat | 6 × | 8–12 |
| Leg Extension (light weight) | 4 × | 10–12 |
| Leg Curl (heavy weight) | 6 × | 10–12 |

# TIM BELKNAP

This huge man burst on the scene in the early 1980s and won the 1981 Mr. America title, which was staged at Caesars Palace in Las Vegas, Nevada.

Belknap weighs a full 220 pounds at a height of only 5 feet 4 inches, with a 21-inch arm. Tim is a diabetic, which is a difficult condition to control under the rigid diet and exercise demands of professional bodybuilding. He is a man of singular perseverance who sees a project through to its climax. In 1984, he made the move from IFBB contests to WABBA competitions where he finished with winning results.

*An incline sit-up . . . Tim Belknap-style*

## Routine

| Monday and Thursday | Sets | | Reps |
|---|---|---|---|
| Hanging Leg Raise | 4 | × | 15–20 |
| Hyperextension | 4 | × | 15–20 |
| Squat | 4 | × | 10–12 |
| Leg Press | 4 | × | 10–12 |
| Leg Curl | 5 | × | 10–12 |
| Standing Calf Machine | 5 | × | 10–12 |

| Tuesday and Friday | Sets | | Reps |
|---|---|---|---|
| Incline Sit-up | 4 | × | 15–20 |
| Bench Press | 4 | × | 4–8 |
| Incline Press | 4 | × | 4–8 |
| Seated Pulley Row | 4 | × | 4–8 |
| Chin | 4 | × | 8–10 |
| Seated Calf Machine | 5 | × | 10–12 |

| Wednesday and Saturday | Sets | | Reps |
|---|---|---|---|
| Roman Chair Sit-up | 4 | × | 50 |
| Seated Press behind Neck | 4 | × | 4–8 |
| Bent Lateral | 4 | × | 4–8 |
| Standing Barbell Curl | 2–3 | × | 4–8 |
| Concentration Curl | 2 | × | 4–8 |
| Lying Triceps Extension | 2–3 | × | 4–8 |
| Standing Dumbbell Extension | 2–3 | × | 4–8 |
| Pulley Pushdown | 3 | × | 6–10 |

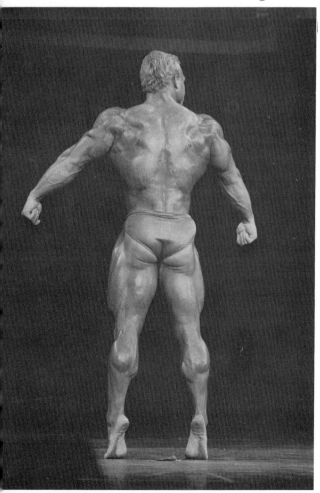

*Tim Belknap*

Tim Belknap

*Roy Callender*

# ROY CALLENDER

A native of Barbados, Roy has spent many years living in London, England, and Montreal, Canada. Currently, he runs a gym in Barbados. Roy astonished the bodybuilding world in 1981 by turning up at Arnold Schwarzenegger's Mr. Olympia presentation in Columbus, Ohio, sporting an incredible physique. However, he didn't win. "They told me if I came in shredded, that I would win the Olympia," said Roy, who existed on egg whites, tuna, skinned chicken, and water during the final weeks of preparation. He certainly looked a winner, but that year the title went to Franco Columbu. Roy will be back.

## Routine

### Day One (Monday)

Calf Raise (all types, but most often the seated version, with extremely heavy weight)
Squat (up to 400–500 pounds)
Leg Press (performed very strictly and slowly)
Deadlift (up to 450 pounds)
High Pull (grip slightly wider than the shoulders)
Weighted Sit-up (3–4 sets)

### Day Two (Saturday)

Incline Dumbbell Press (up to a pair of 150-pound dumbbells)
Incline Flye (up to a pair of 100-pound dumbbells)
Seated Press behind Neck (up to 215–225 pounds)
Side Lateral (cheat reps to get the 80-pound dumbbells up)
Partial Overhead Lateral (up to a pair of 110-pound dumbbells)
Upright Row (narrow grip and strict style with 175–185 pounds)
T-bar Row (up to 280 pounds for 3–4 reps)
Hanging Leg Raise (3–4 sets. For increased resistance, he wears a pair of iron boots or holds a dumbbell between his feet.)

*Roy works his outstanding triceps on a machine.*

*Carolyn Cheshire*

# CAROLYN CHESHIRE

Carolyn Cheshire is Britain's best female bodybuilder. She started training to improve her body while working as a top fashion model. Subsequently, she made such remarkable progress that she was hired by the casting directors of the James Bond movies whenever a perfect body was required. Carolyn trains at Gold's Gym in London and has entered every Ms. Olympia contest since the first event. She is one of the most dedicated bodybuilders in the world.

## Routine

|  | Sets |  | Reps |
|---|---|---|---|
| **Day One** |  |  |  |
| *Chest* |  |  |  |
| Flat Bench Press | 4 | × | 10 |
| Dumbbell Bench Press | 4 | × | 10 |
| Supine Flye | 4 | × | 10 |
| Dumbbell Pullover (across bench) | 4 | × | 10 |
| *Back* |  |  |  |
| Wide-grip Chin | 3 | × | 10 |
| Narrow-grip Chin | 3 | × | 10 |
| Pulldown (in front of neck) | 4 | × | 10 |
| Close-grip Pulldown | 3 | × | 10 |
| Cable Row | 4 | × | 10 |
| Bent-over Barbell Row | 4 | × | 10 |
| Single-arm Row | 3 | × | 10 |
| **Day Two** |  |  |  |
| *Legs* |  |  |  |
| Squat (various foot positions) | 5–7 | × | 15 |
| Leg Press | 5 | × | 15 |
| Leg Extension | 4 | × | 15 |
| Stiff-legged Deadlift (from bench) | 4 | × | 10 |
| Leg Curl (with forced reps) | 4 | × | 10 |
| Toe Raise (on leg-press machine) | 10 | × | 20 |

## Day Three

| Shoulders | Sets | | Reps |
|---|---|---|---|
| Barbell Press | 5 | × | 10 |
| Barbell Front Raise | 3 | × | 10 |
| Lateral Raise | 3 | × | 10 |
| Bent-over Flye (face down) | 3 | × | 10 |
| Upright Row | 4 | × | 10 |
| Dumbbell Shrug (heavy weight) | 3 | × | 10 |

*Carolyn Cheshire*

Carolyn exercises her pectorals with an incline bench press.

| Biceps | Sets | | Reps |
|---|---|---|---|
| Wide-grip Barbell Curl | 4 | × | 10 |
| Reverse-grip Curl | 4 | × | 10 |
| Concentration Curl | 3 | × | 10 |
| *Triceps* | | | |
| Close-grip Bench Press | 5 | × | 10 |
| Lying Triceps Extension | 4 | × | 10 |
| Pressdown | 4 | × | 10 |
| Reverse Pressdown | 3 | × | 10 |
| Cable Kickback | 3 | × | 10 |
| *Abdominals* | | | |
| Weighted Leg Raise | 3 | × | 30 |
| Incline Sit-up (with weight) | 3 | × | 20 |

# CARLA DUNLAP

She's won more professional bodybuilding titles than anyone else. "The mind fails before the body," said Carla, who nevertheless brings an awesome mental concentration and total dedication to her training.

Carla, a former competitive synchronized swimmer, trains very hard and takes no drugs whatsoever. According to training expert Sheila Herman: "You feel like giving up trying to follow Carla through a workout. She moves from station to station without rest. She handles tremendous weights—120-pound seated rows, 60-pound dumbbell rows, 35-pound front raises. . . ."

## Routine

**Day One**

*Back and Shoulders*

| | Sets | Pounds |
|---|---|---|
| Nautilus Lat Machine | 1 × | 80 |
| Close-grip Pulldown | 4 × | 90, 100, 110, 120 |
| Wide-grip Barbell Row | 4 × | 95 to 125–155 |
| Bent Lateral Raise | 4 × | 30 to 45–60 |
| Seated Row | 4 × | 110, 120, 110, 90 |
| Dumbbell Row | 4 × | 50, 55, 60, 55 |
| Deadlift | 4 × | 185, 205, 225, 205 |
| or | | |
| Hyperextension | 4 × | 35–45 |
| Shrug (dumbbell or barbell) | 4 × | 50 or 135 |
| Military Press | 4 × | 80, 90, 80, 70 |
| Press behind Neck | 2 × | 80 |

*A close-grip bench press really stresses Carla Dunlap's triceps.*

| | Sets | Pounds |
|---|---|---|
| Pec-Deck (facing machine) | 4 × | 40, 50, 60, 50 |
| Bilateral Raise | 4 × | 20, 22, 25, 22 |
| Dumbbell Front Raise | 4 × | 17, 20, 22, 20 |
| or | | |
| Barbell Front Raise | 4 × | 30, 35, 35, 30 |

*Waist and Calves* (also on Day Three)

| | | |
|---|---|---|
| Seated Twist | 3–4 × | 50 reps |
| Crunch | 3–4 × | 50 reps |
| Donkey Calf Raise (with 125-pound partner) | 4 × | (to failure) |
| Standing Toe Raise (on block) | 2 × | 260, 280 |
| Standing Toe Raise (on floor) | 2 × | 320, 340 |
| Seated Calf Raise | 8 × | 80, 90, 110, 90 |

## Day Two

*Legs, Biceps, and Abdominals*

| | | |
|---|---|---|
| Full Squat | 4 × | 135, 155, 175, 175 |
| Leg Extension | 4 × | 110, 120, 130, 120 |
| Single-leg Extension | 2 × | 40, 50 |
| Leg Curl | 4 × | 50 (lighter to finish set) |
| Single-leg Curl (each leg) | 2 × | 20 |
| Leg Curl (leg-extension machine) | 3 × | 40, 50, 50 |
| Stiff-legged Deadlift (bench) | 2–3 × | 135 |
| Barbell Curl | 4 × | 55 (lighter to finish set) |
| Incline Dumbbell Curl | 4 × | 22, 25, 30, 25 |
| Reverse Curl | 4 × | 35 (lighter to finish set) |
| Cable Crunch | 3–4 × | 30 |
| Hanging Leg Raise | 3–4 × | 50 reps |
| Dumbbell Twist | 3–4 × | 50 reps |
| Roman Chair Sit-up | 3–4 × | 50 reps |

Carla Dunlap

## Day Three

| | Sets | Pounds |
|---|---|---|
| *Chest and Triceps* | | |
| Incline Barbell Press | 4 × | 95, 105, 115, 125 |
| Decline Dumbbell Press | 4 × | 40, 45, 50, 55 |
| or | | |
| Wide-grip Bench Press | 4 × | 95, 110, 135, 135 |
| Pec-Deck | 4 × | 60, 70, 80, 70 |
| Decline Pullover | 4 × | 50, 55, 60, 65 |
| Cable Crossover | 3 × | 30, 35, 40 |
| Close-grip Bench Press | 4 × | 80, 90, 100, 90 |
| Pulley Pressdown | 2 × | 35, 40 |
| Military Press (reverse grip) | 4 × | 45, 55, 55, 45 |
| Dumbbell Triceps Extension | 4 × | 35–45 |

# CORINNA EVERSON

She's been described as the most genetically endowed person to succeed in women's bodybuilding. And success has already come her way in a clean sweep victory of the 1984 American Championship and the Ms. Olympia contest in Montreal, Canada.

Cory is married to bodybuilding and powerlifting star Jeff Everson and they have appeared in couples contests together. Jeff plans and supervises Cory's training and diet prior to important shows.

## Routine

| Day One | Sets | Reps |
|---|---|---|
| *Chest* | | |
| Bench Press | 1 × | 15 |
| | 1 × | 10 |
| | 5 × | 3–12 |
| Incline Press | 4 × | 6–8 |
| Pec-Deck | 3 × | 10–12 |
| Cable Crossover | 3 × | 10–15 |
| *Shoulders* | | |
| Press behind Neck | 4 × | 6–8 |
| Lateral Raise | 4 × | 8–12 |
| Rear Raise | 4 × | 8–12 |

| Day Two | | |
|---|---|---|
| *Upper Legs* | | |
| Lunge | 4–5 × | 12–15 |
| Thigh Extension | 4 × | 12–15 |
| Leg Curl | 4 × | 12–15 |
| Light Squat | 3 × | 15 |
| *Calves* | | |
| Standing Raise | 3 × | 20 |
| Seated Raise | 3 × | 20 |
| *Abdominals* | | |
| Raises, Crunches, Leg-ups, Twists in a variety of sets and reps. | | |

Corinna Everson

| Day Three | Sets | Reps |
|---|---|---|
| *Abdominals* | | |
| Another session of various abdominal exercises. | | |
| *Arms* | | |
| Dumbbell Curl | 5 × | 12 |
| Triceps Pushdown | 4 × | 8 |
| Pulley Curl | 3 × | 12 |
| Triceps Extension | 3 × | 12 |
| *Back* | | |
| Pulldown | 4 × | 20/15/12/8 |
| Dumbbell Row | 4 × | 10 |
| Close-grip Pulldown (to chest) | 3 × | 12 |
| Long Pulley Row | 3 × | 12 |

*The prize-winning form of a Ms. Olympia—Corinna Everson*

# LOU FERRIGNO

Born in Brooklyn, New York, Lou Ferrigno started training in his early teens. He put on substantial muscle very quickly and competed successfully in IFBB contests. After moving to California to train for the Mr. Olympia contest, he was offered the role of the Hulk in a television series, which ultimately ran for several years. Lou became financially wealthy, and his name became a household word. Lou has made scores of television appearances and several films, among them *Hercules*, in which he appeared as the most massive Hercules ever to be seen on the screen.

Lou is still busy with show-business activities, but he hopes to compete in the IFBB Mr. Olympia—one more time.

## Routine

|  | Sets | Reps |
|---|---|---|
| **Monday and Thursday** | | |
| Sit-up | 1 × | 25–50 |
| Squat | 5 × | 12/10/8/6/4 |
| Leg Extension | 3 × | 8–10 |
| Deadlift | 3 × | 10/8/6 |
| Barbell Bent Row | 5 × | 12/10/8/6/4 |
| Lat Pulldown | 5 × | 12/10/8/6/4 |
| Shrug | 3 × | 10–15 |
| Barbell Curl | 4 × | 10/8/6/6 |
| Dumbbell Curl | 4 × | 10/8/6/6 |
| Wrist Curl | 4 × | 10–15 |
| Standing Calf Raise | 5 × | 10–15 |
| **Tuesday and Friday** | | |
| Leg Raise | 1 × | 25–50 |
| Bench Press | 5 × | 12/10/8/6/4 |
| Incline Press | 5 × | 12/10/8/6/4 |
| Military Press | 4 × | 12/10/8/6 |
| Upright Row | 4 × | 12/10/8/6 |
| Lying Triceps Extension | 4 × | 6–8 |
| Lat Pushdown | 4 × | 6–8 |
| Seated Calf Raise | 5 × | 10–15 |

*Lou "The Hulk" Ferrigno has already won the Mr. Universe title, but he still trains to win the Olympia.*

# BERTIL FOX

This British-born Goliath did not start with the genetic superiority that many people imagine. Bertil trained for many years in a basement gym in London, England. He went on to win the junior Mr. Britain, Mr. Britain, and NABBA Mr. Universe titles. Bertil then joined the IFBB organization and competed in the Mr. Olympia contest. He trains hard and heavy, using cheat movements on many of his exercises. He is considered one of the most awesome bodybuilders of all time. And he still hopes to win the Mr. Olympia title.

*Bertil Fox*

*Bertil Fox*

## Routine

| Monday and Thursday | Sets | | Reps |
|---|---|---|---|
| Incline Sit-up | 3 | × | 20–30 |
| Bench Press | 4–5 | × | 5–8 |
| Incline Press | 3–4 | × | 5–8 |
| Bent-over Row | 4–5 | × | 5–8 |
| Lat-machine Pulldown | 3–4 | × | 5–8 |
| Press behind Neck | 5 | × | 5–8 |
| Upright Row | 4 | × | 5–8 |
| Seated Calf Raise | 5 | × | 10–15 |
| Wrist Curl | 4 | × | 10–15 |

| Tuesday and Friday | Sets | | Reps |
|---|---|---|---|
| Hanging Leg Raise | 3 | × | 15–20 |
| Squat | 5 | × | 5–8 |
| Leg Press | 4 | × | 8 |
| Thigh Curl | 4 | × | 8 |
| Stiff-legged Deadlift | 5 | × | 8 |
| Barbell Curl | 5 | × | 8 |
| Lying Triceps Extension | 5 | × | 8 |
| Reverse Curl | 4 | × | 8 |
| Standing Calf Raise | 5 | × | 10–15 |

# MOHAMED MAKKAWY

It may sound strange, but Egyptian-born Mohamed Makkawy *never* does an exercise unless he has a special reason for doing it.

Each movement serves a purpose. Before a show, Mohamed will analyze the situation. He maintains that physique ideals change periodically. Mohamed will also consider his competition. He will prepare one way to face Lee Haney, another way to face Frank Zane. The following is the routine that he used to prepare for his six winning titles and one second-place finish (the Mr. Olympia) in one year. It is a better record than any other pro bodybuilder has ever done.

*Mohamed Makkawy*

# Routine

| Chest | Sets | Reps |
|---|---|---|
| Bench Press | 5 × | 8 |
| Bench Press (20 degrees) | 5 × | 8 |
| Incline Bench Press (40 degrees) | 5 × | 8 |
| Bent-arm Pullover | 5 × | 8 |
| Wide-grip Dip | 5 × | 8 |
| Straight-arm Pullover | 5 × | 10 |

| Back | Sets | Reps |
|---|---|---|
| High Bench Row | 5 × | 8 |
| Pullup to Waist | 5 × | 8 |
| Wide-grip Chin behind Neck | 5 × | 8 |
| Wide-grip Pulldown to Chest | 5 × | 8 |

| Legs | Sets | Reps |
|---|---|---|
| Hack Squat | 5 × | 8 |
| Seated Pulley Leg Squeeze | 5 × | 10 |
| Thigh Curl | 5 × | 10 |
| Thigh Extension | 5 × | 8 |
| Roman Chair Sit-up | 5 × | 10 |
| Flat Thigh Extension | 5 × | 8 |
| Seated Calf Raise | 5 × | 15 |
| Standing Calf Raise | 5 × | 15 |

Mohamed Makkawy

Mohamed uses a barbell to perform high bench rows.

| Abdominals | Sets | Reps |
|---|---|---|
| Lying Leg Raise | 5 × | 15–25 |
| Hanging Leg Raise | 5 × | 15–25 |
| Hanging Knee-in | 5 × | 15–25 |
| Bent-knee Sit-up | 5 × | 15–25 |
| Twisting Sit-up | 5 × | 15–25 |
| Cross-ankle Crunch | 5 × | 15–25 |

| Shoulders | Sets | Reps |
|---|---|---|
| Wide-grip Upright Row | 5 × | 8 |
| Lateral Raise (45 degrees, facing incline bench) | 5 × | 8 |
| Kneeling Cable Raise | 5 × | 8 |
| Bent-over Cable Raise | 5 × | 8 |
| Lateral Raise | 5 × | 8 |
| Cable Lateral Raise | 5 × | 8 |

| Biceps | Sets | Reps |
|---|---|---|
| Incline Dumbbell Curl | 5 × | 8 |
| E-Z Bar Curl | 5 × | 8 |
| Seated Cable Curl | 5 × | 10 |

| Triceps | Sets | Reps |
|---|---|---|
| Parallel Bar Dip | 5 × | 8 |
| Bent-over Kickback | 5 × | 8 |
| Rope Pull | 5 × | 8 |

Tom Platz

# TOM PLATZ

One of the most popular bodybuilders of all time, Tom Platz is currently the only one famous for gargantuan legs. Tom has also been dubbed the world's hardest-training bodybuilder, and he continues to live up to this title. He seems to continue a set when everyone else would be dropping the weights in agony.

Tom Platz won the Mr. Universe contest, and he still has aspirations of winning Joe Weider's Mr. Olympia title one day. He is among the most well-received of all bodybuilders for guest appearances and seminars.

## Routine

### Monday and Thursday A.M.

| | Sets | Reps |
|---|---|---|
| Dumbbell Bench Press | 12 × | 5–15 |
| Bench Press }superset | 5 × | 5–10 |
| Flye | | |
| Upright Row | 6 × | 8–15 |
| Side Lateral | 6 × | 15–20 |
| Side Cable Raise | 3 × | (to failure) |
| Standing Calf Raise | 4 × | 50 |
| Donkey Calf Raise | 3 × | (to failure) |

*Tom shows championship form in a barbell curl.*

### Monday and Thursday P.M.

| | Sets | Reps |
|---|---|---|
| Chin | 6 × | 15–20 |
| Bent-over Row | 5 × | 10–15 |
| Cable Row | 5 × | 20–25 |
| Dumbbell Pullover | 4 × | 10–12 |
| Press behind Neck | 10 × | 8–10 |
| Bent-over Lateral | 4 × | 10 |

### Tuesday and Friday A.M.

| | Sets | Reps |
|---|---|---|
| Dumbbell Curl | 6 × | 8–12 |
| Close-grip Bench Press | 6 × | 6–10 |
| Strict Barbell Curl | 4 × | 6–10 |
| Pulley Pushdown | 4 × | 10–15 |
| Wrist Curl (on bench) | 4 × | 15–20 |
| Roman Chair Sit-up | 4 × | (to failure) |
| Twisting | 1 × | (10 min.) |
| Crunch (one side at a time) | 2 × | 100 |

### Wednesday and Saturday A.M.

| | Sets | Reps |
|---|---|---|
| Squat (Wednesdays only) | 2 × | 25–50 |
| Hack Squat | 4 × | 2 |
| Thigh Extension | 4 × | 20 |
| Leg Curl | 6 × | 15 |

*Tom squeezes out a pressdown on a lat machine.*

*Gladys Portugues*

# GLADYS PORTUGUES

What a sensation this woman is! Gladys is not only a prize-winning bodybuilder, she is also an enormously popular model in the New York area (she is managed by Better Bodies, 12 W. 21st St., NY, NY).

Much of Gladys's training is done under the watchful eye of Super Fitness gym owner Ken Wheeler, of Toronto, Canada. Gladys won Wayne DeMilia's "Night of Champions" show as an amateur, and she is currently making a success of herself in the professional bodybuilding world. Her goal is to win the Ms. Olympia contest.

## Routine

|  | Sets |  | Reps | Pounds |
|---|---|---|---|---|
| **Monday and Thursday** | | | | |
| *Chest* | | | | |
| Bench Press | 1 | × | 10 | × 95 |
|  | 1 | × | 4 | × 105 |
|  | 1 | × | 6 | × 115 |
|  | 1 | × | 1–3 | × 130 |
| Incline Dumbbell | | | | |
| Press | 1 | × | 10 | × 30 |
|  | 1 | × | 8 | × 35 |
|  | 1 | × | 6 | × 40 |
|  | 1 | × | 1–3 | × 40 |
| Flat Bench Flye | 2 | × | 10 | × 30 |
|  | 1 | × | 8 | × 35 |
|  | 1 | × | 6 | × 35 |
| *Triceps* | | | | |
| Pushdown | 1 | × | 15 | × 50 |
|  | 1 | × | 10 | × 60 |
|  | 1 | × | 8 | × 70 |
|  | 1 | × | 4–6 | × 80 |
| Dumbbell | | | | |
| Extension | 4 | × | 6 | × 40 |
| Parallel Bar Dip (with | | | | |
| weight) | 4 | × | 6 | × 25 |

*(continued on page 184)*

*Gladys has an ideal body from any point of view.*

| Legs | Sets | Reps | Pounds |
|---|---|---|---|
| Squat | 1 × | 10 | × 135 |
| | 1 × | 8 | × 145 |
| | 1 × | 6 | × 155 |
| | 1 × | 4 | × 175 |
| Thigh Extension | 1 × | 15 | × 20 |
| | 1 × | 10 | × 30 |
| | 1 × | 8 | × 40 |
| | 1 × | 6 | × 50 |
| | 1 × | 4–6 | × 60 |
| Leg Curl | 1 × | 10 | × 10 |
| | 1 × | 8 | × 15 |
| | 1 × | 6 | × 20 |
| Standing Calf Raise | 1 × | burn | × 200 |
| | 1 × | burn | × 260 |
| | 1 × | burn | × 300 |
| | 1 × | burn | × 360 |
| Seated Calf Raise | 1 × | 20 | × 100 |
| | 1 × | 20 | × 120 |
| | 1 × | 10 | × 150 |

| Abdominals | Sets | Reps |
|---|---|---|
| Twist | 4 × | 100 |
| Side Bend | 4 × | 100 |
| Crunch | 4 × | burn |
| Leg Raise | 4 × | burn |

## Tuesday and Friday

| Back | Sets | Reps | Pounds |
|---|---|---|---|
| Chins (with weight) | 4 × | 4 | × 25 |
| Barbell Row | 1 × | 10 | × 95 |
| | 3 × | 8 | × 105 |
| Deadlift | 1 × | 10 | × 135 |
| | 1 × | 8 | × 185 |
| | 1 × | 4–6 | × 225 |
| | 1 × | 2–4 | × 235 |
| | 1 × | 1–2 | × 250 |

| Shoulders | Sets | Reps | Pounds |
|---|---|---|---|
| Dumbbell Press | 1 × | 10 | × 30 |
| | 2 × | 6–8 | × 35 |
| | 1 × | 2–6 | × 40 |
| Seated Lateral Raise | 2 × | 15 | × 135 |
| Barbell Shrug | 2 × | 20 | × 145 |

| Biceps | Sets | Reps | Pounds |
|---|---|---|---|
| Barbell Curl | 1 × | 10 | × 50 |
| | 1 × | 8 | × 60 |
| | 1 × | 6 | × 70 |
| | 1 × | 4 | × 80 |
| Preacher Bench Curl | 3 × | 10 | × 40 |

*Abdominals* (same as Monday)

*Gladys demonstrates an incline bench press as Mohamed Makkawy watches.*

# STEVE REEVES

Ever since he won the 1947 Mr. America title, Steve Reeves has become a legend among bodybuilders of the world, primarily because of his magnificent shape. Reeves had a core of fans throughout the world, created even before his long series of Hercules films, because his physique held instant appeal to both men and women. Today he lives happily with his wife, Aline, in California where he breeds Morgan horses.

## Routine

| | Sets | Reps |
|---|---|---|
| *Chest* | | |
| Bench Press (wide grip) | 3 × | 12 |
| Incline Bench Press (45 degrees) | 3 × | 12 |
| *Shoulders* | | |
| Lateral Raise | 2 × | 10 |
| Dumbbell Press | 2 × | 10 |
| *Back* | | |
| Wide-grip Pulldown | 3 × | 12 |
| Seated Pulley Row | 3 × | 10 |
| *Legs* | | |
| Front Squat | 3 × | 15 |
| Leg Press | 3 × | 12 |
| Toe Raise (leg-press machine) | 6 × | 20 |
| *Biceps* | | |
| Incline Dumbbell Curl | 6 × | 10 |
| *Triceps* | | |
| Dumbbell Extension (single dumbbell, lying) | 3 × | 12 |
| Triceps Extension (two-handed, single dumbbell) | 3 × | 10 |
| *Abdominals* | | |
| Leg Raise | 3 × | 30 |

*Steve Reeves's proportionate physique has won him many titles and made him an idol among many bodybuilders.*

*Marjo Selin*

# MARJO SELIN

She hails from Finland and is the Finnish Women's Champion.

Because of her beautiful face and photogenic appearance, she is in great demand for modelling jobs throughout the United States. Marjo has steadily improved her physique through hard training and diet. Marjo works with her husband, Hannu, for the Finnish embassy in Washington, DC.

Her ambition is to one day be crowned Ms. Olympia, which may one day come soon.

## Routine

| | Sets | Reps | Pounds |
|---|---|---|---|
| **Monday** | | | |
| *Abdominals* | | | |
| Sit-up | 3 | × 20 | |
| Roman Chair Sit-up | 3 | × 20 | |
| Incline Leg Raise | 3 | × 20 | |
| *Back* | | | |
| Lat-machine Pulldown | 1 | × 10 | × 150 |
| | 3 | × 4 | × 180 |
| One-arm Dumbbell Row | 1 | × 10 | × 70 |
| | 3 | × 6–8 | × 110 |
| *Chest* | | | |
| Bench Press | 1 | × 10 | × 95 |
| | 1 | × 6 | × 115 |
| | 3 | × 3–4 | × 120 |
| Incline Bench Press | 1 | × 10 | × 95 |
| | 3 | × 8 | × 105 |
| Dumbbell Pullover | 1 | × 15 | × 40 |
| | 3 | × 8–10 | × 65 |
| *Shoulders* | | | |
| Seated Press behind Neck | 2 | × 10 | × 65 |
| | 3 | × 8 | × 85 |
| Upright Row | 1 | × 10 | × 70 |
| | 3 | × 6–8 | × 65 |

*Marjo reps out with upright rows.*

| Tuesday | Sets | Reps | Pounds |
|---|---|---|---|
| *Abdominals* (same as Monday) | | | |
| *Legs* | | | |
| Squats | 1 | × 12 | × 135 |
| | 1 | × 10 | × 155 |
| | 3 | × 6 | × 185 |
| Thigh Extension | 1 | × 10 | × 100 |
| | 3 | × 5–6 | × 180 |
| Leg Curl | 1 | × 20 | × 40 |
| | 1 | × 10 | × 60 |
| | 3 | × 6–8 | × 80 |
| Standing Calf Raise | 5 | × burn | |
| Seated Calf Raise | 1 | × 15–20 | × 90 |
| | 3–5 | × 6–8 | × 160 |
| *Triceps* | | | |
| Seated Dumbbell Triceps Curl | 1 | × 10 | × 45 |

| | Sets | Reps | Pounds |
|---|---|---|---|
| Cable Pressdown | 1 | × 20 | × 50 |
| | 3 | × 8 | × 90 |
| *Biceps* | | | |
| Barbell Curl | 1 | × 10 | × 70 |
| | 3 | × 4–5 | × 100 |
| Close-grip Curl (machine) | 3 | × 10 | × 35 |
| Seated Isolated Dumbbell Curl | 3 | × 8 | × 35 |
| **Thursday** | | | |
| *Abdominals* (same as Monday) | | | |
| *Back* | | | |
| Deadlift | 1 | × 15 | × 135 |
| | 3 | × 10 | × 185 |
| | 3 | × 6 | × 205 |
| Wide-grip Chin | 3–5 | × 8 | |
| Seated Cable Row | 1 | × 15 | × 100 |
| | 3 | × 8 | × 140 |

*(continued on next page)*

Marjo works her biceps with dumbbell curls.

| Chest | Sets | Reps | Pounds |
|---|---|---|---|
| Bench Press | 3 | × 10 | × 105 |
| Inner Pec Press (machine) | 3 | × 10 | × 80 |
| Lateral Cable Pulley | 3 | × 10 | × 50 |
| *Shoulders* | | | |
| Press behind Neck | 3 | × 6–8 | × 40 |
| Upright Row | 3 | × 10 | × 80 |
| Bent-over Rear Deltoid Raise | 3 | × 10–15 | × 15 |

### Friday

| Abdominals | Sets | Reps | Pounds |
|---|---|---|---|
| Crunch | 3 | × 20 | |
| Roman Chair Sit-up with Twist | 3 | × 20 | |
| Leg Raise | 3 | × 20 | |
| *Legs* | | | |
| Hack Squat | 2 | × 10 | × 90 |
| | 3 | × 4–6 | × 155 |

| | Sets | Reps | Pounds |
|---|---|---|---|
| Leg Press | 3 | × 10 | × 290 |
| | 2 | × 6 | × 340 |
| Thigh Extension | 3 | × 10 | × 120 |
| Leg Curl | 3 | × 10 | × 60 |
| Seated Calf Raise | 3 | × 15 | × 115 |
| Donkey Calf Raise | 3 | × 20 | × |
| Toe Press | 3 | × 15 | × 200 |
| *Biceps* | | | |
| Preacher Bench Curl | 1 | × 15 | × 50 |
| | 3 | × 10 | × 65 |
| Seated Isolated Dumbbell Curl | 3 | × 10 | × 30 |
| *Triceps* | | | |
| Seated Dumbbell Triceps Curl | 3 | × 10 | × 60 |
| Cable Pressdown | 3 | × 10 | × 80 |
| Triceps Extension | 3 | × 15 | × 80 |

# DENNIS TINERINO

This bodybuilding superstar has won every major competition except the Mr. Olympia title. To his credit, he is the only major champion to win a steroid-free contest (the Natural Mr. America).

Dennis hails from New York, but he currently lives in California where he is an ordained minister. He enjoys sailing and jazz as well as bodybuilding. While always training for health and fitness, there is a distinct possibility that he will have another try at that elusive IFBB Olympia title.

## Routine

**Monday, Wednesday, Friday**

| | Sets | Reps |
|---|---|---|
| *Back* | | |
| Chin | 6 | × 10 |
| Bent-over Row | 6 | × 6–10 |
| Cable Row | 5 | × 6–10 |
| *Shoulders* | | |
| Press behind Neck | 6 | × 6 |
| Front Lateral | 6 | × 6 |
| Side Lateral | 6 | × 6 |
| *Legs* | | |
| Half Squat | 4 | × 12 |
| Hack Squat | 4 | × 12 |
| Thigh Extension | 4 | × 12 |
| Leg Curl | 4 | × 12 |
| *Calves* | | |
| Standing Calf Raise | 10 | × 10 |
| *Abdominals* | | |
| Leg Raise | 4 | × 50 |

**Tuesday, Thursday, Saturday**

| | Sets | Reps |
|---|---|---|
| *Chest* | | |
| Close-grip Bench Press | 6 | × 6 |
| Decline Dumbbell Bench Press | 6 | × 6 |
| Dumbbell Pullover | 4 | × 15 |
| *Biceps* | | |
| Cable Curl | 6 | × 6 |
| Incline Dumbbell Curl | 6 | × 6 |
| *Triceps* | | |
| Lying Dumbbell Extension | 6 | × 8 |
| Cable Pushdown | 6 | × 8 |

Dennis Tinerino

# INDEX

heavy-and-light routine, 132–133
heavy-duty routine, 102–104
high-rep training, 22–23
Hnatyschak, John, 47*illus.*
holistic routine, 134–135
Homka, Brian, 21*illus.*, 30*illus.*, 59*illus.*, 127*illus.*
Howell, Fred, 118–119
hyperextension, 49, 120

injured-back routine, 116–117
injuries, 48–49
intensity, 14–18, 29–30
isolation exercises, 106
isotension, 66–67

joints, locking, 67
Jones, Arthur, 62, 81, 126
junk foods, 50

Kalas, John, 62
Kawak, Ed, 100*illus.*
King, Jeff, 15*illus.*, 152, 153*illus.*
knee problems, 49, 123

lactic-acid buildup, 64
lateral raise exercise, 57, 134*illus.*
lat pressdown, 181*illus.*
lat pulldown, 44*illus.*, 62*illus.*, 103*illus.*
leg extension, 128*illus.*
Leonard, Gary, 111*illus.*
loading, oxygen, 46
locking joints, 67
low-rep training, 22
Lusko, Cammie, 120*illus.*
Lyon, Lisa, 35

machines, exercise, 26–28
Maille, Andre, 42*illus.*
maintenance training, 105–106
Makkawy, Mohamed, 22, 24, 44*illus.*, 49*illus.*, 64*illus.*, 92*illus.*, 95*illus.*, 102*illus.*, 107*illus.*, 135*illus.*, 144*illus.*, 150*illus.*, 178*illus.*, 179*illus.*
manganese tablets, 118
mass-building routine, 129
McLish, Rachel, 35, 38*illus.*, 60*illus.*, 81*illus.*, 82, 113*illus.*
Mentzer, Mike, 13–14*illus.*, 21, 42, 59, 62, 65, 78–79, 82, 102*illus.*, 103, 132
Mentzer, Ray, 82, 160
Mes, Erika, 16*illus.*, 85*illus.*, 97*illus.*
mesomorphy, 37
Michalik, Steve, 81
milk, 53
Miller, Heidi, 84*illus.*, 99*illus.*
Miller, Joseph A., 41
mitochondria, 23
momentum, 56

Monday-Wednesday, Friday routine, 85–86
multi-angular training, 35
*Muscle & Fitness* magazine, 57
*Muscle Moulding* (Paschall), 34
muscle(s)
  fibre, 16, 23
  length, 37
  priority, 18–19, 73–74
  spinning, 61, 100, 124–125
  tears, 49

nap, midday, 43
natural bodybuilder's routine 111–112
Nautilus, 30*illus.*, 102*illus.*, 126, 127*illus.*, 128
negative reps, 65
nervous system, 42, 43
neurological efficiency, 37
non-apparatus routine, 94–95
Nubret, Serge, 56*illus.*, 103*illus.*, 136*illus.*, 149*illus.*
nutrition, 50–53

off-season routine, 105–106
Oliva, Sergio, 22, 33*illus.*, 35*illus.*, 36, 61*illus.*, 64, 68*illus.*, 99, 114*illus.*, 115*illus.*, 143*illus.*, 156
one-exercise-per-body-part routine, 109
order of exercise, 18–19, 73–74
overenthusiasm, 33
overextension, 39
over-forty routine, 140–141
overload principle, 17–18
over-sixty routine, 141
overtraining syndrome, 41–42
oxygen debt, 31, 64
oxygen loading, 46

P.H.A. routine, 100–101
Padilla, Danny, 22, 159*illus.*
Page, Bruce, 60
Panting, Deanna, 87*illus.*, 113*illus.*, 154*illus.*
parallel bar dips, 102*illus.*, 114*illus.*
Paris, Bob, 11*illus.*, 36, 99, 163*illus.*
Park, Reg, 21, 24–25, 35, 38, 80, 156
partners, training, 43–44, 59
Paschall, Harry, 34, 71–72
pausing, rep, 64
peak contraction, 61–62
peaking, 29
Pearl, Bill, 22–23, 71
Pearson, Tony, 51*illus.*, 74*illus.*, 80, 155*illus.*, 160
pec-deck flyes, 83*illus.*
perseverance, 37–38
Phillips, Val, 78*illus.*
physical culturist, 134
physiological tolerance to exercise, 37
pills, multi-vitamin/mineral, 53
Pirie, Lynne, 62*illus.*
Plakinger, Tina, 51*illus.*
Platz, Tom 66*illus.*, 67, 68, 123*illus.*, 180*illus.*, 181*illus.*

Portugues, Gladys, 24*illus.*, 31*illus.*, 36*illus.*, 44*illus.*, 78*illus.*, 89*illus.*, 95*illus.*, 99, 105*illus.*, 109*illus.*, 118*illus.*, 137*illus.*, 182*illus.*, 184*illus.*
post-exhaust routine, 108
potential, physical, 36
potpourri routine, 114–116
power squat routine, 122–124
power workout, 22
preacher barbell curls, 24*illus.*, 67*illus.*
pre-contest routine, 106–107
pre-exhaust technique, 80–83, 104–105
  for chest, 82, 158
  for lower thigh, 82, 154
  for shoulder, 83, 152
  for upper arm, 146
press, dumbbell, 48*illus.*, 78*illus.*, 89*illus.*
pressdown, on lat machine, 181*illus.*
*Prevention* magazine, 51
priority, muscle, 18–19, 73–74
progressive-resistance principle, 14–16
proportions, physical, 37
*Pro-Style Bodybuilding* (Platz), 68
protein, 52–53
pulldown, lat, 44*illus.*, 62*illus.*, 103*illus.*
pulls, bent-torso, 40*illus.*
pullup, wide-grip, 44*illus.*
pulse, 41–42, 93–94
pumping up, 61, 100, 124–125
pyramid reps, 63

record keeping, 46–48
recuperation, rotation for, 87
Reeves, Steve, 22, 35, 36, 99, 185*illus.*
relaxation, 42–43
reps methods, 54–69
  amount of, 22–24
  burns, 68
  cheat, 57–58
  continuous tension, 67
  cumulative, 58–59
  forced, 59–60
  half, 60–61
  isotension, 66–67
  negative, 65
  pausing, 64
  peak contraction, 61–62
  pyramid, 63
  slo-mo, 62–63
  strict, 55–57
  tempo changing, 69
  "21" system, 69
rest-pause sets, 31, 78–79
Reynolds, Bill, 30, 66, 105
Richards, Frank, 82*illus.*
Richardson, Bill, 67*illus.*
Roberts, Mary, 26*illus.*, 92*illus.*, 156
Roberts, Susan, 57*illus.*
Robinson, Robby, 22, 57*illus.*, 71, 80, 144, 155*illus.*
Ross, Clarence, 38, 156
Ross, Don, 34, 73, 89, 115
rotation for recuperation, 87